★ ★

DEATH OF THE DOLLAR

★ ★

★ ★

DEATH
OF THE DOLLAR

★ ★

PERSONAL INVESTMENT SURVIVAL
IN MONETARY DISASTER

by

WILLIAM F. RICKENBACKER

ARLINGTON HOUSE

New Rochelle   *New York*

FOR T.J.W. AND M.F.W.

fortitudinis causa

Contents

Preface

ONE of the nicest things about doing a book is that it gives you a chance to say thanks in public to some worthy souls. Now that the nag has made it to the finish line, I can give their spurs back to Douglas Johnston of Houston, Robert de Fremery of San Francisco, and Angus MacDonald of Bayport (Minnesota). Donald McLaughlin, chairman of Homestake Mining, kindly offered me some published material I might otherwise have overlooked. The Foundation for Economic Education, Leonard Read commanding, once again allowed me the prowl of its library. My insouciant employer, Wm. F. Buckley Jr., was gratifyingly if suspiciously eager to let me take more time from editorial chores at *National Review*. I express my deep gratitude to Charles de Gaulle, who has recently brought the subject to the attention of the United States monetary authorities.

There is an appendix on monetary reform, not because I wish to emulate the eighteenth-century custom of scribbling constitutions, and surely not because I expect any immediate action, but simply because more than one person who has read the main text has expressed the normal human craving to get a problem solved. For those energetic souls who think all analysis must lead to action, who say: "Agreed we're in a mess, what do you propose?"—for them I offer the few appended remarks. If they should by some mischance fall into the hands of the Secretary of the Treasury, or a relevant congressional committee—why, I suppose no harm's done.

W.F.R.

Briarcliff Manor, N.Y.
25 March 1968

Introductory Note

THE alert reader (and I have no other kind) will notice many passages in the following work that prophesy events that have already come to pass. Lest you harpoon me for sloppy editing, let me explain:

The book was written in the summer of 1967, not to my entire satisfaction but at least within the publisher's deadline. A few weeks went by. It began to appear that the dollar might not be devalued until the end of 1968. I withdrew the book and let it sit. In February 1968 I "rewrote" it by cutting out five impertinent chapters and doing a complete rewrite *ab ovo* of the last chapter.

By now the text already included the fulfilled prophecies. We decided to leave them in, because they establish an informal batting average and allow the reader to weigh the value of the remaining forecasts.

Normally one should be proud of a job that pans out. In this case, when a mere economic journalist, sitting in his house in the woods, working from official publications, foresees a year in advance events that catch the United States monetary authorities by surprise, there is cause only for sadness.

Chapter One

The Great Gold Crisis

IN Karachi, Pakistan, on October 16, 1966, the armed power of the state reached forth and apprehended one Assim Bhatti, aged 50, aboard his yacht, after a chase on the Arabian Sea. Mr. Bhatti, the owner of three mansions in Karachi, an island palace, fleets of automobiles, twelve race horses and seventeen fishing launches, was accused of smuggling gold. Customs policemen had discovered gold worth half a million dollars in one of his residences. It was not the first time for Mr. Bhatti. He had been arrested in 1958, and served three years in prison, after the authorities dredged up a ton and a half of gold from the sea near Karachi, nailing him on a charge of concealing evidence.[1]

In Los Angeles, California, on February 11, 1967, agent Darwin Horn of the United States Secret Service seized and impounded one gold coin belonging to Henry Tedtman, three gold coins belonging to Meyer Berkon, and "several" gold coins belonging to Harold Whiteneck. The three gentlemen, bourse dealers, were attending the convention of the Numismatic Association of Southern California, held at the Statler-Hilton hotel in downtown Los Angeles. Dr. Leland Howard, Director of the Treasury Department's Office of

Domestic Gold and Silver Operations, explained on February 16 that the seizures were quite proper under the regulations pertaining to gold coin jewelry, Section 2:

> In the second category [of coins it is a crime to own] fall coins which have been adapted to a use as jewelry by soldering, drilling, etc., in such a manner as to affect their numismatic value, but which in essence are still coins or, in other words, which can still be extricated from the jewelry item. It does not matter whether these coins could once have qualified as rare, their numismatic value having been impaired. Americans have been prohibited from holding such coins within the United States since 1933 and outside of the United States since 1961. The importation of such pieces into the United States is prohibited, they should be impounded, and a determination as to the disposition to be made of them will be dependent upon the circumstances in each particular case, full details of which should be furnished promptly to this office.

Poor Mr. Berkon, the coin dealer, was frankly amazed. "I don't know the law," he said, "and I am just begging ignorance actually, but I did not know that was the law. I knew coins after 1933 were illegal to have. That I understand, that I knew."[2]

In May 1966 Mr. Paul Friedlander, a reporter with the *New York Times,* addressed the following question to the White House: "Do the trial balloons, the reports and rumors flooding the travel industry about the Government seriously considering restrictions on pleasure travel abroad because of the so-called gold gap—do they represent the thinking of the President?" The White House replied: "No. Furthermore, the rumors did not originate in the Administration."

Nevertheless, within five months it was apparent that the White House or someone exquisitely close to it was indeed profoundly interested in the connection between pleasure travel abroad and the continuing outflow of United States gold. Mr. Charles S. Murphy, chairman of the Civil Aeronautics Board, was scheduled to deliver the opening address at the 36th World Travel Congress of the American Society of Travel Agents on October 10, 1966. The meeting was to be held in Seattle, Washington—home of the Boeing Airplane Company, a manufacturer whose recent products, a series of jet transports, have earned a handsome bit of foreign exchange. Officials of the American Society of Travel Agents made the perfectly normal request that they be given advance copies of Mr. Murphy's speech so that it might be printed and made available in written form to the large group of travel editors and trade press reporters who were expected to attend the convention. Mr. Murphy's office promised that the advance copies would be available on Friday, October 7. The copies failed to arrive.

The officials of the American Society of Travel Agents made a telephone call to Washington. The Civil Aeronautics Board told them the Murphy speech was en route and had been en route for some time. However, it appears that the Civil Aeronautics Board changed its mind rather suddenly. Soon its public relations staff were calling the travel association officials in Seattle and warning them, it is reported, *absolutely* not to allow the contents of the Murphy speech to be divulged until the chairman himself had pronounced his address on Monday. The travel officials began to worry. As things turned out, they had cause for worry. Mr. Murphy concluded his speech with a sour warning that the gold problem was threatening the freedom of international travel:

As you all know, I am sure, the deficit in our international balance of payments continues to be a problem of major proportions. Last year, a large part of the deficit in the travel account stemmed from the fact that [anything originating in Washington stems from the fact that] there were so many more of our residents who flew on foreign-flag carriers than there were foreign nationals who rode on United States flag carriers. It seems to me that the exigencies of the balance-of-payments problem make it necessary for our carriers to get a more equitable share of this business. I realize that your customer will sometimes make a specific request to be booked on a particular airline—be it United States or foreign. However, I would venture the guess that, for the most part, the choice of a carrier is not something that they have given a great deal of thought to— nor something that they have strong convictions about. So I urge you most strongly to do everything you can to sell these people on traveling on one of our United States air-lines.

I might say that I believe it is in the long-run interest of foreign countries, and foreign-flag carriers, to correct the present imbalance in our travel account. Happily, all of us are still completely free to travel abroad, although some of us would be very glad to see more people discovering America instead. But I remind you that there is always the possibility that restrictive steps may have to be taken if the situation does not improve—however distasteful that would surely be for all concerned. We will all be better off if that can be avoided.[3]

In Karachi, in Los Angeles, in Seattle, whether you are an Indian merchant or an American coin dealer or travel agent, you are within earshot of one of the most resounding events of the century: the collapse of the administratively dictated gold standard. You may assume that any event that has such varied and widespread consequences must itself proceed from causes that are many and complex; quite so. It will be the business of this essay to cast some light on this problem of worldwide origin and consequence. And I would beg the attention of all thoughtful people, because there is something other than gold that runs steadily through the three episodes I mentioned at the start. You may have noticed that in each case there was a clear assault on in-dividual freedom. The Karachi merchant had harmed no one; he had only bought some metal; to jail with him. The California coin dealers had harmed no one; they had only mounted some coins as brooches and ear rings; impound their jewels! The travel agents and those who want to go overseas on foreign lines are harming no one; yet the Federal Government warns that this must cease, or "restrictive steps may have to be taken." The question of sound money is of universal interest because the alternative to sound money sooner or later drags in that unplanned consequence, a restriction of individual liberty. Money this or money that is irrelevant; liberty is so far from being irrelevant that a good many people consider it an absolute good.

Now in these three episodes, as in the thousands that could be cited, the constant theme is a shortage of gold—a shortage in the eyes of government officials—which must be made up by squeezing "illegal" gold holdings from the hands of private citizens; or the shortage is conceived as an international imbalance, which may be righted by cajoling or forcing international businessmen to purchase from this country rather than from that.

The United States, for example, has had a deficit in its balance of payments with the rest of the world in every year since 1950, with the single exception of 1957. The accumulated deficit approaches $40 billion—i.e. the dollar value of goods and services supplied to this country by foreigners over and above the dollar value of goods and services we have supplied to them. The deficit thus accumulated has been accounted for in the two classic ways: foreign bankers have accepted payment in gold, reducing the U.S. gold holdings by about $15 billion; or have invested in short-term U.S. notes, so that we now owe about $25 billion on short term.

As a result the United States is technically bankrupt, because its means of payment (about $10 billion worth of gold) is insufficient to pay off its debts (now well over $25 billion). Thus the "crisis" that has attracted the attention of every economist, every major banker, every Congress, every President, and almost every editorial writer of the past five years.

Says the International Economic Policy Association: "In 1964, when the U.S. export surplus reached $6.7 billion, the deficit remained at a $3 billion level, reaching 'crisis' proportions in late 1964 and early 1965."[4]

Economist Sidney Rolfe lays it on the line: "On February 10, 1965, President Johnson sent a special message to Congress on the balance-of-payments problem. In it he rightly emphasized that our over-all economic position is one of strength. Yet the very facts that a special message on the subject is required, that it is coupled with callings-to-Washington of businessmen and bankers, that the meetings are followed by a panoply of 'voluntary' restrictions on the economic activity of the business community with respect to their foreign operations, that the balance-of-payments problem has come front and center in every economic discussion and is the subject of a thousand journalistic alarums, all betray a basic and justified fear."[5]

In October 1965 the National Industrial Conference Board kicked off a series of World Convocations to celebrate its 50th anniversary. For its first conference, held in Tarrytown, N.Y., the Board selected the topic, "Gold and World Monetary Problems."

The great French economist, Jacques Rueff, points out that the political scene has been agitated by questions concerning the balance of payments for a full half-century.[6]

"One of the most serious and pressing economic problems confronting the United States today," commences a thorough academic study issued in 1963, "is the persistent and substantial deficit in its balance of international payments."[7]

The Bank for International Settlements, filing its thirty-fifth annual report in Basle, Switzerland, said in 1965 that the situation remained unsatisfactory. After mentioning some of the steps that had been taken to ease the payments deficit, the bank continued: "If doubts exist on the longer-term efficacy of these measures, as they do, they come from two considerations. First, after the extended series of external deficits, the reserve position of the United States needs to be strengthened to restore full confidence in the dollar. . . . Secondly, it remains a fact that voluntary controls over capital outflows will have to contend with the strong market incentives arising from the continuing disparity in capital availability. . . . Apart from the possibility that market forces may prevail in the longer run, it is also not satisfactory that the distortions implicit in direct controls be allowed to grow or that capital movements be singled out for the main weight of balance-of-payments adjustment."[8]

A year later, in its annual report for 1966, the Bank for International Settlements once again warned about the United States payments position: "Despite substantial progress in some respects, the U.S. balance-of-payments position remained unsatisfactory in 1965. To be sure, the deficit . . . declined. . . . This overall improvement, however, masks the emergence of certain unfavorable developments which may considerably complicate the task of further reducing the deficit in 1966."[9] And again: "In the past ten years there have been important monetary weaknesses to stimulate hoarding. . . . The US payments deficit has also reduced the attractiveness of dollar securities as a vehicle for long-term saving."[10] And again: "With the two reserve centres in external deficit [London and Washington], the reluctance of countries to make commitments on the basic questions leaves an air of unreality in discussions of the problem. . . . A vexing issue also is the appropriate role that gold should perform in the system and the relationship between gold and other forms of reserves."[11]

The New York Federal Reserve Bank, which acts as agent and chief spokesman of the Federal Government in foreign exchange operations, reported in mid-1963 that the "continuing deficit in the United States balance of payments" had resulted in a general weakness of the U.S. dollar in comparison with "most major currencies."[12] Summing up at the end of the year, the New York Federal Reserve Bank said: "The need for continued progress in this direction was indeed becoming more urgent with the passage of time because of the cumulative effects of sustained payments imbalances."[13]

A year later the same official spokesman could report little improvement: "The 1964 United States balance-of-payments deficit continued to be large at $3.0 billion, as against $3.3 billion in 1963, and it was clear that major efforts would still be needed to bring about the required balance. The substantial improvement which began in mid-1963 continued only into early 1964; thereafter the deficit widened again, especially in the fourth quarter. . . ."[14]

Two years after that the New York Federal Reserve Bank was still unable to report any progress. Even the new system of accounting (which will be explained in due course), which reduced the reported deficit, was unable to hide the trend of things: "The United States balance-of-payments deficit on the liquidity basis increased slightly to $1.4 billion in 1966 from $1.3 billion in 1965. . . . Had it not been for a very large shift from liquid to non-liquid investments by foreign monetary authorities and international organizations, a sharp worsening in the payments balance would have occurred."[15]

Even the Federal Reserve Board began to take notice. In October 1964 it described the payments situation in the kind of prose always used by officialdom when a cheery face must be put on to mask a difficulty: "The over-all deficit in the U.S. balance of payments from mid-1963 to mid-1964 was smaller than that for any corresponding period of the preceding 6 years and was less than half the exceptionally large deficit recorded in the period from mid-1962 to mid-1963. . . . For the 12 months ending last June, the deficit on regular international transactions totaled less than $2 billion, as measured by the decline in U.S. monetary reserves, the rise in U.S. liquid liabilities to foreigners, and receipts from special U.S. Government capital transactions."[16]

A year later, in October 1965, the Federal Reserve Board

was positively jubilant: "The international payments position of the United States has improved sharply in 1965 as a result of the response by U.S. banks and other lenders and investors to the President's balance of payments program announced on February 10. In the first half of the year the deficit on regular transactions was at a seasonally adjusted annual rate of $1.3 billion, as compared with deficits of more than $3 billion in each of the preceding 7 calendar years."[17] At the same time, however, a group of international monetary authorities, known as the Group of Ten (see Chapter 3) published the report of their recent meeting. The report, published September 28, 1965, mentioned the great improvement in the U.S. payments position with somewhat more than a grain of salt: "The Ministers and Governors noted in particular that the deficit in the U.S. balance of payments, which had for years been the major source of additional reserves for the rest of the world, is being corrected and that the United States has expressed its determination to maintain [sic: should be: achieve?] equilibrium in its balance of payments. They welcomed this development in the U.S. international payments position. . . . At the same time, they concluded that it is important to undertake, as soon as possible, contingency planning. . . ."[18]

A half-year later the Federal Reserve Board discussed the international payments problem in somewhat more somber tones: "The deficit on the liquidity basis, measured by the decline in U.S. monetary reserve assets and the increase in our liquid liabilities to all foreigners, fell to $1.3 billion in 1965. This was an improvement of $1.5 billion from 1964. On the other hand, on the official reserve transactions basis, which measures the deficit by the decline in U.S. reserve assets and the increase in liquid liabilities and certain non-liquid liabilities to foreign monetary authorities alone, the deficit was also $1.3 billion, but this was little changed from 1964, although it was much smaller than in the years before that. Last year's deficit entailed a large decline in U.S.

gold reserves whereas in 1964 there had been large increases in foreign holdings of dollar assets in the United States, official as well as private."[19]

And, as usual, the international conferences continued to convene to discuss the question of what to do about the monetary situation. On July 26, 1966, the Group of Ten published yet another communiqué after yet another conference in which the perennial sickness of the dollar had been diagnosed: "As regards international liquidity the Ministers and Governors were in full agreement that there is at present no general shortage of reserves. On the other hand, it was thought unlikely that the existing sources of erves would provide an adequate basis for world trade and payments in the longer run. Large U.S. deficits are not a satisfactory source of future reserve increases for the rest of the world; nor are they acceptable to the United States."[20]

In a rare confluence of analytical thought and political tactic, the Republican Party issued a very useful brochure on the gold problem in 1965, whose opening comments were not at all overstated: "The balance of payments problem in the international accounts of the United States, and the outflow of gold from the United States, are symptoms of a danger affecting every American's job and income, the future prosperity of the rest of the world as well as the United States, and, in the larger picture, the question of whether the Free World will maintain [once again: maintain, or acquire?] the economic strength to prosecute and eventually to win the Cold War. Continued failure to deal adequately and promptly with the problem could contribute to a breakdown in the international monetary system with the possibility of bringing to the United States and other free nations a depression of serious proportions and duration. In such circumstances, everyone would suffer."[21]

The problem of the payments imbalance was tracked fairly clearly by commercial banking circles also. The comments over the years of the First National City Bank are typical.

In March 1959 the bank noted presciently: "We have entered an era of sharper competition in world markets. More and more people, here as well as abroad, are wondering whether the U.S., because of its high production costs, is losing its position in world trade—'pricing itself out of world markets.' . . . To maintain its position in export markets as well as to hold respect for the dollar, the U.S. will need to guard against wage-price spiraling. Government outlays abroad, and continuance of private capital exports, must have a counterpart in merchandise exports, competitively priced. Otherwise, the result is gold outflow, from a substantial though not inexhaustible stock, or a further increase in U.S. short-term indebtedness to other countries."[22]

The bank resumed its discussion within a few months, in July 1959: "Once again there is much comment, here as well as abroad, about the decline in the U.S. gold stock. . . . The size of the gold outflow is less a matter of concern than developments in the balance of payments that give rise to a deficit of the present magnitude. There has been this year a further fall in merchandise exports and a continuing rise in imports."[23]

The bank returned to the theme in 1960: "In a world in which market mechanisms—prices, exchange rates, and interest rates—are working once more, the long insulation of the United States from the discipline of the balance of payments has come to an end. Today, the United States, however richly endowed and productive, can no longer conduct its domestic financial affairs without regard to its ability to supply goods and services at competitive prices, to maintain interest rates in line with those in the principal markets abroad, and to preserve a feeling of complete confidence in its currency by its own people as well as by foreigners."[24]

Late in 1960 the question was up again: "Gold has figured increasingly in the news in recent months . . . [there are] two fundamental considerations. One of them is the persistence, for a third consecutive year, of a $3-billion-plus deficit in

the U.S. balance of payments. . . . Secondly, there are fears,
expressed by some Americans and foreigners alike, that a
new Administration taking office January 20 next will enlarge
government spending and perhaps also seek to impose an
artificial cheap money policy [it did just that]. . . . We must
be watchful of our international solvency. . . ."[25]

In December 1960 the bank noted that we still had enough
gold to cover our net short-term liabilities, but that we
should mend our ways: "Our international financial position,
while not as dominating as ten or fifteen years ago, remains
strong enough to give time for needed policy adjustments."[26]

The new Kennedy Administration introduced a brilliant
assortment of technical responses to the payments problem,
with the result that the gold outflow came to a halt in the
early months of 1961—temporarily, as it turned out. The
First National City Bank correctly assessed the situation in
mid-1961: "The balance-of-payments deficit, dramatized by
the fall in the U.S. gold stock, has given rise to a great variety
of plans and proposals for specific changes in our institutions,
policies, and practices—ranging from special bonus interest
rates for foreign central banks to limitations on U.S. imports.
The rub is that we cannot deal with fundamentals by tech-
nicalities and improvisations; nor should we wish to set
precedents for a new wave of trade restrictionism. The
urgent need of the moment—to safeguard the dollar—is to
exercise self-restraint and avoid the quicksands of inflationary finance."[27]

A year later, towards the end of 1962, the bank once again
downgraded the merely technical tactics of the new Administration: "Adjustments of the kind needed to redress the
U.S. balance of payments necessarily take time. The dollar
is not yet like Caesar's wife—above suspicion. . . . Ingenious
new exchange techniques, including borrowings of international reserves, may be helpful to support each other's currency. They do not, however, touch the roots of international
imbalance. They can spare a currency the manifest symptoms of weakness in exchange markets. They will be posi-

tively harmful if, through their technical success, they distract attention from fundamentals."[28]

Commenting early in 1963 on the suggestion that private American investment overseas was the cause of the dollar outflow, the bank said: "The balance-of-payments deficit has not resulted in a loss of our international weath. . . . Yet, the strength of our international balance sheet must not make us complacent about the major job that remains to be done to bring our international payments into better order . . . we can succeed only if we safeguard the real value of the dollar—measured, as it must be, by what it will buy in commodity markets and earn in investment markets."[29]

In 1964, as there had been many times in the past, there was a flicker of hope. Indeed, the deficit on international account had acquired the quality of the deficit on domestic account. Just as every President and every Congress for the past generation had praised the balanced budget even while running almost continuous deficits for more than thirty years, so now every President at least once a year was telling Congress how important it was for the United States to balance its international accounts even while that balance remained forever deferred. The First National City Bank was beyond optimism by February 1964: "As President Johnson noted in his Economic Message, the deficit in the U.S. balance of payments—though 'still with us'—has been reduced 'sharply.' This is most heartening, since the large and stubborn payments gap has long cast a shadow over the dollar. . . . The decline in the U.S. balance-of-payments deficit may be creating the impression that the United States is, at long last, rounding the corner. Any conclusion of this sort, however tentative, would be premature."[30]

Premature indeed. By the end of 1964 the long history of monetary illness produced another warning signal in domestic finance. (An earlier signal was the Presidential prohibition on American citizens' purchase or ownership of gold in foreign countries—raising interesting and unanswered questions as to the limits of Executive decree.) The problem had

to do with the gold reserve ratio—the legal requirement that
the Federal Reserve System maintain its gold reserves at
no less than 25 per cent of the total value of its outstanding
notes and liabilities. No new gold was coming into the
System, and at the same time the Federal Reserve was
issuing new notes (much of them in order to replace silver
certificates) and extending new credit to the banking system.
What with the perennial loss of gold and the accelerated
issue of Federal Reserve notes, we were beginning to scrape
the bottom of the barrel. The First National City Bank reported on the new situation: "As 1964 is shaping up, the
U.S. balance-of-payments deficit—as conventionally defined
—may be something like $2-2.5 billion, compared with $3.3
billion in 1963. . . . Reconsideration of the gold reserve requirement seems forced by circumstances. . . . It is indisput-
able that protection of the gold reserve should be a prime
objective of U.S. Government actions and policies."[31]

I trust the point is sufficiently clear. Observers foreign and
domestic, governmental and private, are unhappy with the
manner in which the U.S. has conducted its financial affairs.
The problem is by common acknowledgement extremely
serious, but men of sound mind may not agree on calling it
a crisis. A crisis is a moment in which a choice must be made.
The U.S. gold situation has been, up to now, an *era* in which
a choice must be made. In 1959 the First National City
Bank was thankful to note that our position was so strong
that we had time to consider what steps we should take
to shore up our payments balance; in September of 1966
an important New York banker made exactly the same
remark.[32] Knowledgeable observers have been pointing at
the problem for eight years. Certainly it is a crisis inasmuch
as the necessity for making ultimately a real choice is obvious and the consequences of that choice will be felt around
the world.

The problem, as seen from Washington, is that foreign
bankers are holding such a large total of claims against the

U.S. that if they presented them all at once we would be unable to pay them off, as we have promised to pay them off, in gold. This would involve the U.S. in a repudiation of a series of promises that have formed the basis of the monetary systems of half the nations of the world.

As foreigners see it, the problem is that they hold "assets" that are perhaps only half-assets: a promise is, after all, no better than the actual probability of its being made good. If it is perfectly clear that the U.S. cannot honor all of the promises it has outstanding, then how good is A's claim or B's claim against the U.S.? Yet A and B and many others have deposited those claims in their own official banking systems, treated them as assets, counted them as financial reserves, and then in turn issued their own promises to their own citizens—"backed" by the questionable promise of the U.S.! America's international insolvency places the internal solvency of many foreign countries in question.

The facts and figures are published regularly and are available to anyone who cares to pay a visit to his local bank or library. The following report on the monetary gold stock is taken from a recent *Federal Reserve Bulletin*.

Gold Stock	($ billions)
1941 (Dec.)	$22.8
1945	20.0
1950	22.9
1956	21.9
1957	22.8
1958	20.6
1959	19.5
1960	18.0
1961	16.9
1962	16.0
1963	15.6
1964	15.4
1965	13.8
1966	13.2
1967 (Feb.)	13.1

No statistician could ask for a cleaner trend line. Simply laying a pencil along the plotted numbers, you can foresee that the United States will be devoid of gold within twenty years. But the end will come sooner than that, because there is a characteristic acceleration towards the end of long-term monetary cycles. More and more people notice that a certain thing is happening, more and more people take evasive action, and that very action of evasion accelerates the monetary movement. In this case a faster flow of funds from dollar areas to other areas must be foreseen. It will intensify the burden of foreign banking circles who hold dollar claims they're not sure of. The accelerated accumulation of dollar claims in their hands will lead much sooner to the showdown over the ability of the United States to meet its obligations. You could look forward to this much at least, if the only figures you had at your disposition were the figures of the U.S. gold holdings.

If, on top of these figures, you also had the figures on our growing indebtedness, you would begin to share some of the sense of urgency that is the most remarkable common feature in expert appraisals. You would have noticed that in the early 1950s our short-term liabilities to foreigners were only about $5 billion—about one-fourth of our gold reserve. You would have watched our short-term debts climb to $26 billion in 1963, $28.9 billion in 1964, $29.1 billion in 1965, $31.4 billion at year-end 1966. It would become clear to you that we are now far below water as far as our ability goes to pay off our short-term obligations in the coin of the international realm, i.e. gold. It should be clear that something must give way, or a great break is in the offing. In the space of barely more than a dozen years we have gone from the point where our gold stock was four times our short-term debts—to the present, when our short-term debts are three times our gold stock. This ominous trend has set in despite the pronounced intentions of every President and Congress, despite the expert maneuvering of monetary technicians, despite exhortations and special pieces of legislation. Something much stronger than politics is at work. The laws of economics are at work, and I surely believe we must make our obeisances to those laws sooner or later. We shall make our obeisances pleasanter if sooner, harsher if later. But sooner or later we shall be forced to act. Then the crisis, the time of choosing, will be upon us.

Will we choose a money system worthy of a free people, or will we protect ourselves behind a wall of legal measures such as Finance Minister Schacht built for the Hitler regime? As an earnest partisan of individual liberty, I can only say that I hope that the Great Society will know how to avoid Hitlerism.

Notes

1. *New York Times*, Oct. 17, 1966.
2. *Coin World*, March 1, 1967.
3. *New York Times*, Oct. 16, 1967.
4. *The United States Balance of Payments*, copyright the International Economic Policy Association; Washington, D.C., 1966.
5. *Gold and World Power*, by Sidney E. Rolfe; Harper, 1966; p. 1.
6. *Le lancinant problème des balances de paiements*, by Jacques Rueff; Paris, Éditions Payot, 1965; p. 13.
7. *The Dollar Crisis*, by Fatemi, Saint Phalle, and Keeffe; Fairleigh Dickinson University, 1963; p. 1.
8. *Thirty-Fifth Annual Report*, Bank for International Settlements; Basle, Switzerland, June 1965; p. 6.
9. *Thirty-Sixth Annual Report*, Bank for International Settlements; Basle, Switzerland, June 1966; p. 6.
10. Ibid., p. 35.
11. Ibid., p. 175.
12. *Monthly Review*, Federal Reserve Bank of New York, July 1963, p. 104.
13. *Annual Report, 1963*, Federal Reserve Bank of New York, p. 11.
14. *Annual Report, 1964*, Federal Reserve Bank of New York, p. 33.
15. *Annual Report, 1966*, Federal Reserve Bank of New York, p. 31.
16. *Federal Reserve Bulletin*, October 1964, p. 1233.
17. *Federal Reserve Bulletin*, October 1965, p. 1367.
18. Ibid., pp. 1407, 1408.
19. *Federal Reserve Bulletin*, April 1966, p. 456.
20. *Federal Reserve Bulletin*, August 1966, p. 1149.
21. *The Balance of Payments, the Gold Drain, and Your Dollar*, published by Republican National Committee; Washington, D.C., 1965.
22. *FNCB Monthly Letter*, March 1959, p. 32.
23. *FNCB Monthly Letter*, July 1959, p. 80.
24. *FNCB Monthly Letter*, May 1960, p. 59.
25. *FNCB Monthly Letter*, November 1960, p. 127.
26. *FNCB Monthly Letter*, December 1960, p. 138.
27. *FNCB Monthly Letter*, July 1961, p. 81.
28. *FNCB Monthly Letter*, September 1962, pp. 105, 107.
29. *FNCB Monthly Letter*, March 1963, p. 35.
30. *FNCB Monthly Letter*, February 1964, pp. 18–19.
31. *FNCB Monthly Letter*, December 1964, pp. 136–138.

32. Mr. Sidney Homer, of the great bond house of Salomon Bros. & Hutzler, in a speech before the National Association of Business Economists, Washington, D.C., September 29, 1966: ". . . our balance sheet is too strong [sic] that we can well afford many mistakes. . . . The asset side of [the U.S.] balance sheet is unbelievably large and is still growing far faster than the liability side."

★ ★ ★ ★ ★ ★ ★

Chapter Two

★ ★ ★ ★ ★ ★ ★

Money Managers
to the Rescue

As you might expect, a problem that has attracted the attention of the civilized world for the better part of a decade will also have given rise to remedial action. The money managers have not been inactive. They have been ineffective, for the deficit is still with us—as, indeed, some of us prophesied it would be, no matter what steps the money managers might take, for just so long as those steps did not include any progress towards balanced budgets at home.

I

To be specific: over the years the various Administrations in Washington have taken some two dozen steps in response to the problem of the ineradicable international deficit.[1]

1. In October 1959 the Development Loan Fund began to concentrate on financing the export of U.S. products to needy countries. (I.e. if Emergent Nation A can buy a product cheaper in some other country, we'll pay A a little extra

if it will spend the money in the U.S. This gives rise to several undesirable side-effects. Though we pay extra in foreign "aid," Nation A is no better off. We make an enemy of the nation with lower production costs; naturally it will accuse us of "dumping." Through the subsidy, our domestic capital is encouraged to remain invested in uneconomic (i.e. high-cost) operations. The dangerous precedent of using "foreign aid" as a clandestine technique for subsidizing American industry is established. Does this explain why so very few American businessmen are on record against "foreign aid"?)

2. Starting in 1960 the International Development Association urged other countries to share the U.S. burden of helping the newly emerging nations. (Successful, to some extent; our allies, especially West Germany, have been quite active in charitable works; but U.S. foreign aid has not been reduced by the amount our allies' aid has increased.)

3. In November 1960 the Defense Department got orders to reduce the number of family dependents of military and civilian Defense personnel overseas, and to reduce overseas procurement. (Cost in terms of morale overseas, unknown; additional transportation cost of shorter overseas tours, unknown; effect on re-enlistment rates, unknown; actual effect on balance of payments, minimal; effect on total cost of procurement, inflationary.)

4. In November 1960 the International Cooperation Administration was directed to place primary emphasis on financing goods and services of U.S. origin. (I.e. Federal subsidies to U.S. exporters are "International Cooperation." Like Step #1 above, this step, if successful, achieves nothing but the appearance of improvement—rather like putting rouge on the cheeks of the dying. In the long run such steps are counter-productive. To wit: if the Federal Government were willing to run a domestic deficit of $30 billion a year in order to subsidize the export of U.S. goods at unrealistically low prices, our "trade balance" would show a fine sur-

plus, it is true; but the consequent inflation would greatly undermine the buying power of the dollar; so that foreigners would have less and less reason to purchase U.S. goods that were unsubsidized. Off at the end of the process we would have total subsidy and total collapse.)

5. In November 1960 the State Department stores and commissaries were forbidden to purchase certain foreign goods. (Total saving, minimal; effect on State Department operating expenses, inflationary; diplomatic effect, awkward.)

6. Starting in 1960 the Defense Department reduced by $40 million the amount of foreign-produced goods it buys for resale in post exchanges. (Here the subsidy to U.S. manufacturers is routed through the Pentagon as conduit; once again the "exports" show up on the balance-of-payments reports, but the hidden cost is unstated. Another example of window-dressing that is, over the long term, counterproductive.)

7. In 1961 the "Buy American" program went into effect in a big way. Under this program the amount of subsidy to U.S. industry was stated explicitly. The Defense Department was to do its buying from U.S. sources rather than foreign sources if the U.S. prices were not more than 25 per cent *higher* than the foreign competition. In July 1962 the subsidy threshold was raised to a full 50 per cent! By that time, most other agencies of the Government were authorized to use the same differential in their own procurement programs. (Effect: alienate foreign producers; raise Federal expenditures; subsidize uneconomic producers at home; habituate American industry to Federal handouts.)

8. On November 19, 1964, the Defense Department announced the "consolidation, reduction, or discontinuance of 15 overseas activities—hospitals, food depots, radar traffic control, etc." (If military operations are obviously wasteful, Congress should investigate and punish the officers responsible; if they are not wasteful, then the society that cannot afford its own defense is not long for this world.)

9. "Department of Defense made special reviews of essentiality of overseas construction, emphasizing use of U.S. contractors, materials, carriers, prefabricated installations and structures, and available troop labor." (It is impossible from the language to know whether the first function of the Defense Department is military or monetary. Why, at additional cost, should Defense "emphasize" the subsidy of U.S. exports?)

10. In 1964 the Defense Department limited offshore procurement in military assistance programs to commitments already on the books. (More of the same.)

11. In 1963-1965 the Defense Department continued to bear the brunt of the payments problem. It cut down on overseas personnel by shortening supply routes; reduced overseas headquarters staff; reduced employment of foreigners overseas; consolidated (reduced?) the B-47 bomber force; and leaned more heavily on the military capabilities of other countries. (A layman cannot judge the precise effect of such moves; but the general presumption is still valid that a country should be able to afford the kind of military structure its *military* officers recommend.)

12. Starting in 1961, the Defense Department and the Treasury Department persuaded foreign countries to buy military equipment from U.S. producers in order to offset U.S. military expenses in those countries. West Germany has collaborated most notably in this program—though not without complaints that she could buy the goods cheaper elsewhere. Starting in February 1965, Australia and Britain increased their military procurement in the U.S. Such exports now run about $1 billion a year. (Is this not extortion? If U.S. products were attractively priced, foreign countries would buy them as a matter of common sense. Instead, we seem to be forcing them to buy, under the threat of withdrawing our military forces. Yet the justification for U.S. overseas military force is that it is in *our* best interest also . . .?)

13. Beginning in August 1961, the U.S. borrowed from foreign official institutions in order to forestall their purchase of gold. Since the borrowings were repayable in dollars, the problem of overseas dollar glut was merely deferred. Treasury Under Secretary Robert Roosa corrected that deficiency by arranging, in October 1961, that future borrowings be repayable in foreign currencies. (Borrowing to cover a deficit is by definition no solution of the deficit. Repaying the loan in a foreign currency can be accomplished only if the foreign currency is acquired through further borrowing, sale of gold, or payments surplus. Borrowing to pay off loans incurred to cover deficits is hardly sound. Selling gold to pay off loans incurred to save gold is folly. The payments balance is as far from surplus as it ever was.)

14. Starting in October 1962, time deposits of foreign governments and foreign financial institutions in U.S. banks were exempt from limitations on interest rates paid. (I.e. the American banks were forbidden to pay to Americans as high an interest rate as they paid to foreigners. The hope was that we could compete for liquid funds in the international market by upping the interest rate, while maintaining low interest rates at home in the belief that cheap money would stimulate the economy. Consequence: liquid domestic capital will try to invest in foreign situations that permit it to enjoy the benefits of the higher rates paid on foreign deposits in American institutions. An expansion of domestic capital outflow will be installed—see Step 25, below. At the end, if nothing stops the process, capital export will be prohibited.)

15. An "interest equalization tax" on acquisitions by Americans from foreigners of foreign debt and equity securities was proposed in July 1963 and became law in September 1964. It was extended to bank loans with maturities of one year or more in 1965. (The prohibition of capital export. If Step #14 above ratifies high overseas interest rates, and if Americans are forbidden to enjoy those rates at home, they

will seek to invest overseas. But Step #14 is supposed to make capital flow toward these shores, not away. Therefore it is necessary to keep Americans from investing overseas. Outright punishment would be Hitlerian. Slapping a special tax on a certain activity is the American way of achieving the same thing. The additional investment income earned on securities in high-interest foreign markets is taxed away by special discriminatory legislation—the Interest Equalization Tax. Effects: American capital forbidden to seek most efficient uses; overseas interest rates protected from American competition; world capital markets narrowed; sense of justice dulled by one more unopposed example of discriminatory legislation; small results in balance of payments.)

16. In 1961 the Treasury ceased to handle international gold transactions directly; the job went to the Exchange Stabilization Fund. In 1962 the Federal Reserve System went into similar operation. (The purpose was to conceal from public view the short-term movements of gold, which would be apparent, and would be the subject of commentary, week by week as the Treasury issued its weekly report. If, instead, the Exchange Stabilization Fund handled the gold transactions, the Treasury need report no change in its gold holdings during normal weeks while the Stabilization Fund's holdings were fluctuating; the Treasury would report changes in gold holdings only when it made a transfer to the Stabilization Fund. What countries were taking our gold, and on what kind of schedule, could become apparent only in the broadest general outline. Basically such a policy of concealment is a magic operation in Voegelinian terms; out of sight, out of mind, what the public doesn't know won't hurt it, and if no one talks about the problem then it will go away.)

17. From 1962 onward, foreign governments were urged to repay their debts to the U.S. on an accelerated schedule. They did so, in significant amounts; France especially—about which more in Chapter 3. (A program clearly available only

once; the sign, indeed, that we were running out of expedients.)

18. Special arrangements were made for borrowing from the International Monetary Fund (a separate chapter below).

19. Starting in 1962, the Treasury entered into various agreements with foreign central banks for "currency swaps" —a form of short-term borrowing of foreign currencies to meet unusual demands for such exchange. (No more eloquent measure of the dollar's position in international finance is needed. From this time on, the dollar was not to be considered as a prime means of international settlements. Bankers preferred other currencies. And we borrowed those other currencies in order to make payments.)

20. The Export-Import Bank in 1962 was added to the general picture of export subsidies when it initiated a program to finance exporters and to provide political risk insurance.

21. In 1964 the financial resources available to the International Development Association (a subsidy conduit: see Step #2 above) were increased.

22. In 1961 the International Travel Act was signed into law. Its purpose was to promote tourism in the U.S. by foreigners (to bring us foreign exchange) and by Americans who might otherwise go abroad (and spend foreign exchange). The program has not been remarkably successful. There is some indication that it, too, has been counterproductive: i.e. a certain number of Americans have decided to go abroad sooner rather than later, in the fear that the U.S. will impose travel restrictions, exchange controls, or other prohibitions. See Step #23 below.

23. In 1961 the duty exemption on foreign purchases by U.S. citizens returning from abroad was reduced from $500 to $100. In 1965 it was recommended that it be reduced further to $50. (Insignificant in dollar amounts; a nuisance tax; regressive; and extremely bad in terms of international

and domestic public relations—i.e. the possible harbinger of even more restrictive policies.)

24. In February 1965 the Federal Reserve Board issued "guidelines" for the foreign lending activities of U.S. banks, establishing so-called "voluntary" limitation of such lending activity to no more than 5 per cent above the preceding year. (A very ominous prelude, some thought, to eventual control over capital exports.)

25. Also in February 1965 the Department of Commerce asked American businesses to accept "voluntary" reductions in direct investments abroad, to increase exports, reduce imports, and increase the use of U.S. flag carriers. This led to such strange locutions as the threat to "impose" even more "stringent" "voluntary" controls over the foreign activities of American business.

26. Simultaneously the President sought, and the Congress granted him, authorization to liberate the Federal Reserve System from the legal requirement that it hold gold reserves equal in value to 25 per cent of the combined liabilities and Federal Reserve Notes outstanding. This "gold reserve ratio" had been reduced from 40 per cent to 25 per cent after the Second World War in order to ratify the great inflation that had occurred during the early 40s. In the succeeding twenty years two factors—the decline in the gold stock and the swelling of Federal Reserve Notes and liabilities—combined to drive the ratio down to the danger level around 27 per cent. The Government at this point had the choice of ceasing the inflation or altering the gold reserve requirement. It compromised by removing the liabilities from the requirement but keeping Federal Reserve Notes subject to the 25 per cent gold cover. Said cover jumped immediately to 42 per cent; but, such was the volume of Federal Reserve Notes printed (chiefly to replace Silver Certificates, which were being withdrawn in order to release the silver stockpile for market price suppression),

within two years the gold reserve ratio for Notes alone was striking down towards 30 per cent. Presumably the gold linkage to Federal Reserve Notes will soon be cut, and then we shall have a monetary system totally bereft of any built-in warning system.

II

Another line of defense was statistical. It would not be accurate to say that the Federal Government invented three different ways to view the deficit, or to view the accounting problems involved in the balance of payments; but certainly the Treasury Department was alert to the opportunities for confusion that were implicit in the rather academic discussions over balance-of-payments accounting.

For a long time the Government had described its payments position on the "basic transactions" model. This was acceptable as long as things were going fairly smoothly. However, by 1963 we were running sizable deficits according to that system of measurement; and so the Treasury shifted over to a different scheme, the "overall position." This system included features quite repugnant to common sense. Under criticism, the Administration scurried to yet another accounting mode, the "regular transactions" description. That system gave way to the "official settlements" concept. Recently we have been hearing of the payments balance "on a liquidity basis."

Perhaps the simplest way to illustrate the differences in these various budgetary concepts would be to study a recent actual year—we'll take 1964—from these different points of view.

Basic Transactions Concept
U.S. Balance of Payments for 1964
($ millions)
1. Balance on goods and services, except
transfers under military grants   8,209

2. Remittances and pensions, net   −830
3. U.S. Government grants and capital, net, except military grants and advance repayments of U.S. Government loans   −3,705
4. U.S. Government nonliquid liabilities, net, except those in lines 8b and 8c   255(a)
5. U.S. and foreign direct investments, net   −2,271
6. Other U.S. and foreign long-term capital, net, except foreign holdings of marketable U.S. Government bonds and notes   −1,829
7. BALANCE ON "BASIC" TRANSACTIONS (sum of items above; equal, with opposite sign, to sum of items below)   −171
8. Special Government transactions: (b)
    a. Advance repayments of U.S. Government loans   122
    b. Advances on U.S. military exports, net   206
    c. Sales of U.S. Government nonmarketable, medium-term, nonconvertible securities(c)   −36(d)
9. BALANCE ON "BASIC" TRANSACTIONS AND SPECIAL GOVERNMENT TRANSACTIONS(e) (sum of items above; equal, with opposite sign, to sum of items below)   121
10. U.S. private short-term capital, net   −2,107
11. U.S. private short-term commercial and brokerage liabilities, net   118
12. Net errors and omissions   −893
13. U.S. liquid liabilities including U.S. Government nonmarketable, medium-term, convertible securities   2,590
14. U.S. monetary reserve assets, including gold, convertible currencies, and IMF position [increase=(−)]   171

(a) Includes purchase by the Government of Canada of $204 million of U.S. Government nonmarketable, me-

dium-term, nonconvertible securities in connection
with transactions under the Columbia River Treaty.
(b) U.S. Government nonmarketable, medium-term, convertible securities are shown in the SCB as special
Government transactions, and shown further, in alternative treatments, as either liquid or nonliquid
liabilities and are not counted as special Government
transactions.
(c) Includes Export-Import Bank portfolio fund certificates of participation.
(d) Excludes securities described in footnote (b) above.
(e) Corresponds approximately to "balance on goods and
services, Government assistance, and long-term capital
accounts" shown in the SCB, Table 2, line C. The
figures differ somewhat because in the SCB table, U.S.
Government grants and capital have been reduced,
and outflows of U.S. private short-term capital have
been increased, by the amount of U.S. Government
aid used by foreigners to repay private U.S. credits.

Thus the "basic transactions" account of our international
payments. The most distinguishing feature is that it treats
short-term capital movements "below the line"—i.e., not as if
they were factors contributing to our deficit or surplus, but
as if the deficit or surplus arose from more "basic" business
and the short-term capital movements were a response to,
and a way of financing, the deficit or surplus. The difficulty
is that short-term capital can react consistently according
to long-term trends, in which case it should be treated no
differently from long-term capital.

Another treatment of the balance of payments is the so-
called "liquidity" basis. The year 1964, on this basis, looks
rather different:

Liquidity Concept
U.S. Balance of Payments 1964
($ millions)

1. Balance on "basic" transactions	−171
2. U.S. private short-term capital, net	−2,107

3. U.S. private short-term commercial and brokerage liabilities, net   118

4. Net errors and omissions   −893

5. BALANCE ON REGULAR TYPES OF TRANSACTIONS, i.e. on transactions other than special Government transactions and changes in U.S. reserve assets and in U.S. liquid liabilities (sum of items above; equal, with opposite sign, to sum of items below)   −3,053

6. Special Government transactions   292

7. BALANCE ON ALL TRANSACTIONS OTHER THAN CHANGES IN U.S. RESERVE ASSETS AND IN U.S. LIQUID LIABILITIES (sum of items above; equal, with opposite sign, to sum of items below)   −2,761

8. U.S. liquid liabilities including U.S. Government nonmarketable, medium-term, convertible securities   2,590

9. U.S. monetary reserve assets, including gold, convertible currencies, and IMF position [increase=(−)]   171

The outstanding feature of the "liquidity" approach is that it aims to describe changes in the U.S. position as world banker—changes, i.e., that affect the U.S. ability to honor its pledge to redeem foreign dollar claims in gold at $35 an ounce. Consequently any additions to U.S. liquid liabilities are treated "below the line" as an inflow of financing to offset the payments figures; whereas U.S. short-term loans overseas are treated as current deficits on the ground that they constitute potential claims on our gold. This system probably tends to overstate a current deficit. It is also subject to the same criticism that we have made of the "basic transactions" concept: it distinguishes too sharply between long-term capital and short-term capital.

The third major concept of international accounting is the "official settlements" method. This method was recommended to the Commerce Department by the Review Committee for Balance of Payments Statistics (1965: the "Bernstein" Committee, after its chairman) and is favored by most international institutions.

Official Settlements Concept
U.S. Balance of Payments for 1964
($ millions)

1. Balance on "regular types of transactions"	−3,053
2. U.S. liquid liabilities to:	
a. Foreign official nonmonetary institutions	....
b. Foreign commercial banks	1,415
c. International nonmonetary institutions	−246
d. Private nonbank foreigners	348
3. Advances on U.S. military exports(a)	206
4. U.S. Government nonmarketable, medium-term, nonconvertible securities sold to the Swiss Confederation	30
5. Less: U.S. Government nonmarketable, medium-term, nonconvertible securities sold to the Government of Canada in connection with transactions under the Columbia River Treaty	204
6. BALANCE SETTLED BY OFFICIAL TRANSACTIONS (sum of items above; equal, with opposite sign, to sum of items below)	−1,504
7. Special intergovernmental transactions: advance repayments of U.S. Government loans	122
8. BALANCE SETTLED BY RESERVE TRANSACTIONS (sum of items above; equal, with opposite sign, to sum of items below)	−1,382
9. U.S. liabilities to foreign official monetary institutions	1,211
a. Liquid liabilities	1,073
b. U.S. Government nonmarketable, medium-term, nonconvertible securities sold to foreign official monetary institutions	138

10. U.S. monetary reserve assets, including gold,
convertible currencies, and IMF position
[increase=(−)]   171

This method makes a distinction between private and
official (monetary institution) ownership of foreign short-
term capital invested in dollar securities. To the extent that
foreign private short-term capital can be withdrawn just as
readily as official reserves, the distinction is overly tran-
quilizing. On the other hand, it is perfectly true that some
large portion of foreign private short-term capital stays on
hand in U.S. banking institutions as a form of collateral for
commercial loans—and is therefore hardly to be considered
a sign of weakness.

The point of this glance at the varying ways to account
for international balances is that no single system answers
all needs. The "basic transactions" system of accounts provides perhaps the clearest view of long-term underlying
trends in our international position. The "liquidity" concept
is of course the best tool for measuring current changes in
our position as an international banker. The "official settlements" method seems peculiarly well designed to measure
the real size of the U.S. imbalance (whether surplus or
deficit) in relation to the imbalances reported by our major
trading partners.[2]

The most important thing to derive from this excursion
into accounting practices is that no matter which approach
you take, you will find that the U.S. has been in deficit on
international account for the better part of twenty years—
and that all of the gimmicks and window-dressing since
1960 have utterly failed to get to the bottom of the problem.

III

Just as we have seen how the developing U.S. deficit did
not escape the observation of interested experts, so we

notice we are not alone in remarking on the peculiar ineffectiveness of the past seven years' efforts to "cure" the deficit, to stop the outflow of gold. In this connection the running commentary of the Bank for International Settlements is most instructive:

June 1959: "The fact that such a considerable proportion of the total volume of liquidity consists of liabilities of the United States and the United Kingdom implies that the working of the system of international payments depends at present to a large extent on the pursuit by these countries of economic and monetary policies aimed at maintaining the purchasing power of their monetary units, and so preserving confidence, both at home and abroad, in their currencies. . . . It must always be borne in mind . . . that the raison d'être of international liquidity is to cover short-term balance-of-payments fluctuations and that to increase it can never be an alternative to sound domestic economic policies, which are the essential condition of any real external monetary equilibrium."[3]

June 1960. "Despite the expansion in trade, it cannot be said that the volume of international liquidity . . . is at present inadequate. But its structure is worthy of attention. From the end of 1949 to the end of 1959 the part consisting of gold holdings increased from $35.4 milliard to $40.7 milliard, that consisting of sterling from $8.8 to $9.8 milliard and that consisting of dollars from $6.0 to $16.2 milliard, or from 12 to 24 per cent of the total. This rise in dollar balances [the foreign analogue of the U.S. payments deficit], a large proportion of which are in fact held by Europe, has provided a useful addition to international liquidity, but at the same time it brings with it certain responsibilities. For one of the conditions for the smooth working of the system is that the holders of these balances should feel it to be in their interest to retain them. Here again the main responsibility rests with the United States, which must itself ensure that international confidence in its currency is maintained and also that the conditions offered to foreign holders are sufficiently attractive."

June 1961. ". . . policy measures must include further balance-of-payments improvements among their objectives. . . . The problem is not one of a shortage of international liquidity. . . . Nor is it one of an inherent defect in the present monetary system. The problem is one of allaying nervousness and of strengthening confidence in major currencies. The solution lies, above all, in restoring a reasonable basic equilibrium in balances of payments. This is certainly not an easy matter, but if it is neglected no palliative can be successful."

June 1962. "The objectives of the [U.S.] government include safeguarding the dollar without import restrictions or exchange controls, maintaining adequate forces overseas, keeping to foreign aid commitments and continuing domestic recovery. These goals taken together are not an operating policy because they do not specify an order of priorities and because they may implicitly restrict possible action to put a given priority into effect. Balance-of-payments developments over the past year indicate a need for a higher priority on achieving a fairly rapid decline in the external deficit; while the attainment of full-employment levels of domestic activity remains a fundamental need of the American economy, the pace of further expansion (whether spontaneous or policy-stimulated) must be consistent with and guided by rapid progress on external account . . . it is not appropriate that the combination of policies followed on both sides of the Atlantic should be encouraging a net flow of capital towards Europe which has to be financed by U.S. gold losses and the piling up of short-term dollar liabilities . . . such losses of gold by the United States and accumulation of short-term dollar holdings by other countries cannot continue indefinitely . . . it should be emphasised that, for certain products important in international trade, U.S. prices remain significantly higher than European prices. For such

products, stability is not an adequate objective. . . . The best
way to ensure that the inevitable fluctuations in balances of
payments remain within reasonable bounds is for each country to keep the internal purchasing power of its currency as
stable as possible."

June 1963. "The U.S. authorities have tried, in a variety
of ways and with a moderate degree of success, to reconcile
the opposing policy requirements of the external deficit and
unused domestic resources. It is evident, however, that the
situation calls for more vigorous measures. . . . The basic
problem in international payments has not been liquidity,
therefore, but balance-of-payments disequilibrium—persistent in the case of the dollar . . . it is not facing reality to
look for the cause of the trouble in the international financial
system as such, or to imagine that it can be solved by easy
access to international liquidity. . . . As a whole, however,
the result has been to prolong the deficit. While much in-
genuity has been shown in maintaining the international
position of the dollar and protecting it against speculation,
there is evident need for more basic action."

June 1964. "The interest equalisation tax must be seen
as an expedient to cover an underlying disequilibrium between the United States and the outside world. . . . It
matters little whether one considers that the economy is not
competitive enough with respect to goods or too competitive
with respect to money; on one side or the other the adjustment process must continue in the years ahead. . . ."

June 1965. "The programme to correct the [U.S.] external
deficit was limited for several years to the following measures: tying foreign economic aid so as to reduce the free
dollars sent abroad; securing economies in defence outlays
abroad and arranging offsetting defence purchases in the
United States, particularly by Germany; and restraints on
wage costs and prices to improve the competitive position
of domestic industry. In addition, various techniques were
used to hold up short-term interest rates despite the policy

of monetary ease, in an attempt to discourage the net out-flow of short-term funds. . . . Since the authorities were directing general fiscal and monetary policy towards domestic objectives, it became necessary to secure balance-of-payments equilibrium by unorthodox means. This background led to the second policy experiment, the interest equalisation tax. . . . By mid-1964 . . . it was clear that the interest equalisation tax had failed to stem the outflow of private U.S. capital. . . . Hence, the problem of securing a more fundamental equilibrium still remains. . . . In the past few months the payments imbalance between the United States and Europe has been considerably lessened—as a direct result of the voluntary restraint programme in the United States as well as of special measures in various continental countries to limit the inflow of capital. While one can see the necessity at times for using such direct steps to keep control over capital flows, one must be concerned about these limitations on free convertibility. It is not only that their effectiveness could weaken after a time but that they imply that capital flows, more so than other elements in the balance of payments, are the appropriate route for adjusting overall imbalances. Hence, there is a danger of growing distortions if the underlying disequilibrium in interest rates and the availability of capital funds is neglected. In the United States the active domestic expansion generated by the tax reductions gave the opportunity for tighter monetary policy to help the external position, but little was done along this line."

June 1966. "For most industrial countries of Western Europe, as well as for the United States, the economic situation at the present time is one of excessive demand and pressure on prices. . . . The situation has been better in that the deficits of the United States and the United Kingdom have been reduced. As this was accomplished in large measure by the action of direct controls, however, the need for adjustment of underlying market forces remains pressing. . . .

Despite substantial progress in some respects, the U.S. balance-of-payments position remained unsatisfactory in 1965. To be sure, the deficit (as computed according to the 'liquidity' concept) declined by $1.5 milliard to $1.3 milliard. . . . This overall improvement, however, masks the emergence of certain unfavourable developments which may considerably complicate the task of further reducing the deficit in 1966. . . . One may conclude that on both sides of the Atlantic national authorities have come to rely increasingly on selective measures that enlarge the scope for independent monetary action. . . . The drawback on such selective techniques lies in their susceptibility to prolonged retention. Once imposed, they weaken the link between the external payments position and the appropriate policy mix. In so far as the domestic scope for monetary policy is widened, the pressure to act in the fiscal and incomes fields is accordingly reduced. In the case of deficit countries, in particular, the extended reliance on selective measures is analogous to having unlimited access to international reserves and credit facilities. Thus, the danger is that, instead of trying to reconcile its various policy goals, a country will tend to neglect basic external adjustment. While such an outcome is not inevitable, the danger is a real one. . . . The sharp deterioration in the U.S. balance of payments in the second half of 1964 had increased uneasiness about the dollar. And these doubts were intensified by the widely publicised French decision to convert part of the country's exchange reserves into gold and by official French statements in favour of a return to the gold standard. Against this background, reassurances by the United States that the dollar's existing gold parity would be maintained, action to abolish the statutory gold cover for the Federal Reserve System's deposit liabilities and the announcement of the voluntary balance-of-payments restraint programme did little to dispel nervousness."

It is instructive to examine any question from more than

one side. In this case we should turn next to the Federal Reserve Bank of New York, which is the Federal Government's principal agent in dealing with foreign exchange and the forces of the international monetary world. On April 22, 1963, Mr. Alfred Hayes, President of the Federal Reserve Bank of New York, delivered an address before the Economic Club of New York in which he attempted to rebut the criticisms of the Swiss bankers: "I have heard," he said, "our swaps and foreign currency borrowings criticized as 'cover ups' that cause us to lose sight of the underlying need for payments equilibrium; but I can assure you that neither the Treasury nor the Federal Reserve has had the slightest illusion that they are in any sense a substitute for the needed remedial actions. Rather, apart from their longer term value as a contribution to world liquidity, they serve at present as a holding operation while we undertake, by more fundamental measures, to get our basic payments deficit under control."[4] The verdict of five more years is now in: Mr. Hayes was fibbing, and the Swiss analysis was correct.

Towards the end of 1963 a very interesting paper was published under the joint authorship of C. A. Coombs of the Federal Reserve Bank of New York, M. Iklé of the Banque Nationale Suisse, E. Ranalli of the Banca d'Italia, and J. Tuengeler of the Deutsche Bundesbank. These bankers noted the urgency of the dollar problem: "Quite clearly, the United States Government has given the only answer to one horn of the liquidity dilemma by asserting its firm determination to close the United States balance-of-payments deficit. Failure to do so would have disastrous consequences extending far into the future. While some progress toward reducing the deficit was made in 1961 and 1962, the time factor has now become a matter of major importance [1963!]."[5]

Late in 1963 the New York Fed disclosed, even through the normal opacity of official prose, the degree of concern among the world's bankers: "A series of actions to reinforce the international payments mechanism through cooperative measures has, of course, been taken over the last few years. Furthermore, the mechanism has been under constant study and review by a number of official bodies, including the IMF [International Monetary Fund], the central bankers who meet regularly at the Bank for International Settlements in Basle, Working Party 3 of the Economic Policy Committee of the Organization for Economic Cooperation and Development (OECD) in Paris (which deals particularly with financial policies of member countries), and national treasuries and central banks . . . the central bankers emphasized that even strong currency defenses cannot be a substitute for the eventual correction of major underlying payments imbalances—a point heavily stressed at the IMF meetings as well. In this respect, the continued balance-of-payments deficits of the United States have been a source of concern."[6]

The system of currency swaps that had been set up early in 1962 reached maturity in 1964. As of August 31, 1964, the Federal Reserve enjoyed swap agreements with twelve foreign central banks or official institutions, the smallest of which involved $50 million. These arrangements can be summarized as follows:

Institution	Amount of Facility ($ millions)	Term of Arrangement (mos.)
Bank of France	100	3
Bank of England	500	12
Netherlands Bank	100	3
National Bank of Belgium	50	6
Bank of Canada	250	12
Bank for International Settlements	150	6
Swiss National Bank	150	6
German Federal Bank	250	6
Bank of Italy	250	6

Austrian National Bank	50	12
Bank of Sweden	50	12
Bank of Japan	150	12
	2,050	

Through mid-1964 the Federal Reserve had had occasion to draw on every bank listed with the exception of the Bank of Sweden. The total of such drawings was $1.803 billion, and all but $65 million had been repaid.

Six months later, on March 1, 1965, the swap arrangements had been expanded further, and the term of repayment had been extended in two cases (Belgium and Italy).

Institution	Amount of Facility ($ millions)	Term of Arrangement (mos.)
Bank of France	100	3
Bank of England	750	12
Netherlands Bank	100	3
National Bank of Belgium	100	12
Bank of Canada	250	12
Bank for International Settlements	150	6
Swiss National Bank	150	6
German Federal Bank	250	6
Bank of Italy	250	12
Austrian National Bank	50	12
Bank of Sweden	50	12
Bank of Japan	150	12
	2,350	

While arranging these agreements for reciprocal and short-term currency borrowings, the U.S. Government was simultaneously issuing long-term bonds denominated in foreign currencies—i.e. borrowing with the promise to repay not gold or dollars but foreign exchange. By March 3, 1965, these debts totaled more than a billion dollars' equivalent:

United States Treasury Bonds
Denominated in Foreign Currencies
March 3, 1965

Issued to	Amount (millions)	
	Foreign Currency	U.S. dollar equivalent
Austrian National Bank	2,600 Austrian schillings	100.6
National Bank of Belgium	1,500 Belgium francs	30.1
German Federal Bank	2,700 German marks	679.0
Swiss National Bank	1,112 Swiss francs	257.5
Bank for International Settlements	300 Swiss francs	69.5
		1,136.7

In March 1965 President Johnson's Administration gave signs of extreme activity. Commerce Secretary John Connor issued a letter to 600 business executives asking them to take action to reduce the payments deficit. He also asked them to initiate the filing of a new form report, quarterly, relating to their international activities. "I am sure you are aware," his letter concluded, "of the vital importance of improving the United States balance-of-payments position. Such improvement is essential to international monetary stability, to this Nation's economy, and to continued business progress. The capability of this Nation to manage its international fiscal affairs is being carefully watched around the world. President Johnson is confident, as am I, that you will cooperate with us in this extremely important program of serious concern to you and to our country. We urgently need your help." Nothing much ever came of this program, naturally.

By September the swap network had expanded further, to $2,800 million, and the U.S. was using swaps at a new high rate. Foreign currency bonds issued by the Treasury increased by $122 million, and further drawings were made from the International Monetary Fund.

On October 27, 1965, Mr. Alfred Hayes, President of the Federal Reserve Bank of New York, delivered an address on the general subject of international finance and in it felt constrained to describe, within the limits of official English, the vast failure of the monetary authorities to do anything about the payments problem. "While international payments equilibrium has been a recognized goal of official United States policy for five or six years, it has not been the only goal of policy, and the attainment of the balance of payments goal has indeed been elusive. There are few who would deny that our large-scale deficits have continued much too long."[7]

Early in 1967 Mr. Hayes showed little desire to rhapsodize over the progress forever deferred: "No review of the problems we face can neglect our balance of payments and our international position generally—an area which is a matter of deep concern. . . . Unfortunately, achievement of balance in our external accounts will be anything but easy."[8]

In 1966, for the first time in recorded history, the monetary gold stocks of the civilized world declined. Although there was evidence that the sum of hoarding also declined slightly, still the largest factor in private buying of gold remained hoarding, either for speculative purposes or in order to protect financial assets from the losses that arise when currencies depreciate.

The United States payments deficit remained unbudged during 1966 and U.S. official gold reserves declined by $400 million. The currency swap system was enormously expanded:

Federal Reserve Reciprocal Currency
Arrangements and Commitments
February 28, 1967

Institution	Amount of Facility ($ millions)
Austrian National Bank	100
National Bank of Belgium	150

Bank of Canada	500
Bank of England	1,350
Bank of France	100
German Federal Bank	400
Bank of Italy	600
Bank of Japan	450
Netherlands Bank	150
Bank of Sweden	100
Swiss National Bank	200
Bank for International Settlements	400
	4,500

Dr. Walter Spahr of the Economists' National Committee on Monetary Policy has summed up very nicely the official juggling of gold statistics—a juggling act that goes hand in hand with other deceptive practices that are indulged in in order to tranquilize or bamboozle the monetary world. Says Spahr: "In its weekly *Condition Statement of F. R. Banks*, the Federal Reserve authorities report only Treasury stock as 'gold stock.' Furthermore, as of Wednesdays, the figure on gold stock is frequently juggled for the day by a shift of gold, at least in the figures, from the Exchange Stabilization Fund to Treasury gold stock. Thus the figure on 'gold stock,' (Treasury gold stock) for the report day (Wednesday) can appear better than the figure for 'the week ended' on Wednesday or for the preceding Wednesday. After the window dressing for Wednesday, the window-dressing part of 'gold stock' can be, and often is, returned to the Exchange Stabilization Fund. Still further, a pronounced loss of gold during a week (from Wednesday to Wednesday) has frequently been made to appear smaller than the fact of the loss, through juggling the figures between the Exchange Stabilization Fund and Treasury gold stock (called 'gold stock' in the weekly statement), by distributing the loss through two or more weekly statements. Thus the weekly Federal Reserve statements on 'gold stock' can readily mislead those who do not follow with understanding and care the weekly and monthly pertinent data."[9]

IV

A vintage example of leak, cover-up and half-news came to light in April 1967. As background I might mention that in mid-March Mr. Henry Fowler, the Secretary of the Treasury, made a speech in which he indirectly threatened that the U.S. would consider putting a stop to all gold payments unless foreigners come up with stronger support for the dollar. Well:

In the first week of April 1967 spokesmen from two eminent banks on opposite shores of the country, the Chase Manhattan and the Bank of America, almost simultaneously came out and suggested that in a showdown "the dollar is superior to gold and that the United States need not be so 'defensive' about the deficit in its balance of payments."

A newspaper article on April 11 carried on: "Government officials have reacted with keen interest to unexpected statements last week by the Chase Manhattan Bank and the Bank of America. . . . Although men in Government are cautious about discussing this delicate subject, the following points can be stated on good authority: The Government neither wants nor expects a showdown or crisis, which would take the form of a 'run' on the United States gold stock. . . . However, there is a deep awareness in the Government of the underlying strength of the dollar. . . . It is not too much to say that the men in charge believe, like the two large commercial banks, that in a showdown over which is worth most, the dollar would win and gold would lose, even though no showdown is expected. . . . If there ever were a crisis, in the form of a run on the gold stock, the United States would suspend gold payments. . . . A deeply involved high official has said, 'We have looked into the eye of the storm we think will not come, and we have unanimously decided that an increase in the price of gold would not be our defense.' The Government still considers the balance of payments problem an important one. . . ."[10]

On the same day, the Chase Manhattan Bank issued a
statement denying that it had advocated any policy change:
". . . no change in the official price of gold is necessary or
desirable, now or in the future. The possibility of ceasing
the purchase or sale of gold in a time of crisis is also a course
fraught with great risk and uncertainty. . . . In citing that
approach as a possible consequence of a monetary crisis, no
implication should be read into the . . . analysis that a
change in our gold policy is in any sense advocated."[11]

The news story went on: "According to both sides, the
two private bank statements were not inspired or suggested
by the Government, despite some natural suspicions at home
and abroad . . . the statements were not even inspired by
each other, having occurred by coincidence in the same
week."

Thus the *New York Times*. On the very same day the
event was treated, with interesting differences, in the *Wall
Street Journal*. Herewith some excerpts from the *Journal*
story: "The U.S. Government appears to be making a mo-
mentous switch in its strategy for defending the stability of
the dollar . . . it's believed the Treasury has quietly notified
foreign nations that if they buy too much gold from the
dwindling U.S. reserves, the U.S. may refuse to sell them
any more gold—even if it still has some left to sell. Within
the last few days the nation's two largest banks, Bank of
America in California and Chase Manhattan in New York,
have advocated precisely this step. Their statements, though
presumably prepared a continent apart, developed the same
detailed argument for a change in U.S. gold policy and in
key sections were nearly identical in wording. Both the
banks and the Treasury deny that the banks were floating
a trial balloon for the Johnson Administration. Indeed, the
Treasury issued a statement yesterday saying . . . that 'there
is no contemplated change in U.S. policies toward the buying, selling, or price of gold.' . . . Despite this statement,
there is good reason to believe that the banks' policy views

came as no surprise to Treasury Secretary Henry Fowler and were not unwelcome to him. . . . The U.S. has made innumerable ringing declarations that it will never devalue the dollar, but Mr. Deaver [the Chase Manhattan vice president who wrote the controversial article] and others believe foreign nations—and perhaps some Americans—have never been absolutely convinced. . . . Even before Mr. Fowler spoke at Pebble Beach the Treasury had received assurances of one sort or another from Canada, Britain, Japan and Italy that those nations would try to avoid buying U.S. gold for a while. The Administration is known to be trying now to wring a pledge from West Germany that it won't buy any U.S. gold for a year. . . . These views . . . have upset the New York Federal Reserve Bank, which has the duty of actually dealing with foreign central banks. But it is believed the Chase—Bank of America ideas have met with approval at the Federal Reserve Board in Washington and are not unwelcome at the White House either."[12]

A fantastic turn in this little mystery story came the very next day. The American Bankers Association repudiated the statements of the Chase Manhattan and the Bank of America. A senior officer of the Bank of America repudiated the ABA repudiation. The Treasury denied everything: "The Treasury Department, in a formal statement, has disavowed any connection with the statements last week by the Bank of America and the Chase. Moreover, a spokesman for the department said yesterday it would be incorrect to read into a major policy speech last month by Secretary of the Treasury Henry H. Fowler at Pebble Beach, Calif., any inference that a change in gold policy was being considered. Senior officials of both the Bank of America and Chase conferred with Mr. Fowler at the Pebble Beach meeting. . . . But despite this denial, as well as similar denials from the two banks that their original statements had been inspired in Washington, the feeling persists in banking circles that some change in this country's gold policy is being con-

templated. In the meantime, informed bankers say that
European central bankers, whose institutions are major
holders of dollars that could be converted into gold, are
deeply disturbed by the reports of a possible change. 'The
animals are stirring,' said one highly placed banker yesterday. . . . In an attempt to stave off gold drains, the Government has been imposing increasingly stringent controls over
foreign lending and investing by American business."[13] [This
last remark is the first public notification I know of that the
"voluntary" system was a flop, and has been converted into
a system of stringent government controls.]

Finally, a news report of April 13: "London, April 12.—
The price of gold jumped sharply in the London market
today because of exceptionally heavy demand. Some an-
alysts thought the brisk buying was linked to uncertainty
about United States gold policy. . . . The curious thing about
today's gold market was that everyone seemed to know
vaguely, but no one precisely, why there were new grounds
for confusion about the United States gold policy. . . . News
dispatches from Washington indicated that there had indeed
been a distinct modification of the Treasury's traditional
willingness to sell gold to foreign governments. Treasury
officials, the reports disclosed, were at least discussing the
possibility that in the event of a run on American gold reserves, the Treasury might stop selling gold for a time despite its official denial of any change in policy."[14]

It may be months or years before we know what really
happened. Did Fowler intend to urge a U.S. embargo on
gold payments? Did he put the bee in Chase's ear? Were
Chase and Bank of America acting in concert? Did President Johnson tip his hand? Why did Chase issue a retraction
that retracted nothing? Which Treasury official admitted
that a change had already been agreed upon—"unanimously"? You should not attempt to follow the fortunes of
the United States Treasury Department unless you have a
distinctly developed taste for soap opera.

In sum, the Money Managers have reacted very amateurishly to the challenge of the international monetary problems. I can do no better than to quote Sidney Homer once again:

The weakest spot has been the contrast between our words and our deeds. We have repeatedly announced programs which would end our payments deficit and we have been repeatedly disappointed. This gives the impression that we have lost control. If we could once clearly demonstrate control of our deficit, we could thereafter better afford deficits. The term 'deficit' is merely an ugly, inaccurate word for a further growth in the bank's deposits.

Over five years ago a great President referred to our gold exports as a hemorrhage which must and would be stopped. It was not stopped. . . .

Like any bank the confidence of our depositors is the foundation stone of our banking structure. Confidence is achieved usually by action in silence, but where explanations and promises are called for the explanations must be candid and the promises must be exceeded.

Nevertheless, over and over again in the last six years we have first announced a crisis in our balance of payments, then proclaimed action which would end the crisis, then given out optimistic progress reports, and finally confessed to a shortfall. All this has been only a well intentioned demonstration of very bad public relations. If we had not in fact been drawing on vast resources, the result should have been calamitous. Silence would have been far better. [Do you hear, Joe Fowler, do you hear?]

Today we blame the deficit on Vietnam, but the dollar drain from Vietnam can be no surprise. A while ago we blamed it on the vast foreign investment plans of American corporations, but could they have been a surprise? Then we blamed it on the British crisis, but was that a surprise? Now we blame it on imports caused by a domestic boom but were they unexpected? When the guidelines were revised last January, most of these contingencies might have been known and more than allowed for. Instead the world was told that our deficit would be ended by late 1966, but now there is silence on that point.[15]

Let us turn now to a closer look at the institutional framework of the international monetary system. It is obvious that the U.S. authorities have no understanding of the situation; that is no reason for the average citizen to infer that it's too hard to comprehend. And first: the IMF.

Notes

Chapter 2.

1. *The Gold Situation;* committee print for Legal and Monetary Affairs Subcommittee of House Committee on Government Operations; Washington: July 1965; pp. 27–28.
2. International Economic Policy Association, op. cit., p. 159 ff., is my principal source in this discussion.
3. The following quotes come from the relevant annual reports of the Bank for International Settlements.
4. NYFRB *Monthly Review,* May 1963, p. 71.
5. Ditto, August 1963, p. 115.
6. Ditto, November 1963, p. 167.
7. Ditto, November 1965, p. 223.
8. Ditto, February 1967, p. 24.
9. *Monetary Notes,* January 3, 1967 (Economists' National Committee on Monetary Policy, 79 Madison Ave., NYC).
10. *New York Times,* April 11, 1967, p. 63.
11. Ditto, p. 69.
12. *Wall Street Journal,* April 11, 1967, pp. 1, 21.
13. *New York Times,* April 12, 1967, pp. 65, 71.
14. *New York Times,* April 13, 1967.
15. Op. cit.

Chapter Three

The Failure of the International Monetary Fund

THE chief institutional expression of the present arrangements for international settlements is the International Monetary Fund. Along with the World Bank (properly, the International Bank for Reconstruction and Development) the IMF was set up in 1944 as a result of the notable Bretton Woods conference (New Hampshire). In order to understand the present system it is necessary to understand the IMF. To understand the IMF it is necessary in turn to know something of the developments leading up to the Bretton Woods conference.

The world monetary system has gone through four phases, if I may be permitted to speak in global generality. The first phase lasted from prehistoric times down to about 1800. It was a system in that it operated to facilitate international trade and payments; it was no system in that it was not the creature of a conference, a government, or an individual, but was the spontaneous organic answer to a need. Though there were thousands of different kinds of money circulating, they were almost all in the form of coin, and almost all coin contained some portion of rare metal, usually gold or silver. A merchant who desired to do business in a foreign market would have to acquire a coinage that circulated in that market. He might take a sum of his own coinage to that market, exchange it for the going coinage on the basis of equal metallic content, and go about his business. Or he might, in a more advanced area, acquire the foreign currency by patronizing the money-changers—merchants whose sole business it was to provide a market in foreign exchange. It was this type of specialist whom Christ cast out of the temple.

Towards the end of the eighteenth century Great Britain emerged as a world center of trade, commerce, commodity markets, and banking. Also, as the center of the first extensive colonial empire, Britain found that her banking system was called upon to act as an international medium. Thus, with central banking itself hardly a century old at that point, the world moved into the second phase of international monetary arrangements: the gold standard. Britain's currency was convertible into gold at a fixed rate for foreign and domestic holders alike; and the central bank stood ready to buy or sell gold at the fixed price. Deposits in London banks financed trade among countries other than Britain. The advantages to London were tremendous. By the end of the nineteenth century the whole civilized world was operating more or less on the gold standard, in which metallic gold and the British pound were the universal terms of monetary measurement.

The First World War put an end to the easy and automatic international convertibility of currencies under the gold standard. Phase Three commenced, characterized by governmental interventionism, a great loss of flexibility and freedom in trade, and a retreat into forms of mercantilism and isolationism not seen for centuries. Foreign deposits during war were blocked. War imports took first place; exports must be controlled lest they help the foe. Governments take over control of the mechanism by which one currency is exchanged for another; thus the governments control almost the whole of the balance of payments. Phase Three is called the gold/exchange standard, because the international reserve unit was now not only gold but also foreign exchange: i.e. a bank might count among its reserve assets not only gold (the exclusive reserve under the gold standard) but also its holdings of foreign currencies which are in turn convertible (in international settlements) into gold. Under the straight gold standard any net surplus or deficit in the balance of payments would be settled by gold shipments, and to some extent the country exporting gold would feel a deflation and the country importing it an inflation. If these monetary forces were allowed to work their whole effect, the price levels in various countries tended to move towards the point where trade would be in balance. By the 1920s, however, the feeling was widespread that it was more important to avoid deflation than it was to stabilize the monetary system. So the full arsenal of wartime monetary powers was moved over to peacetime conditions. Exchange controls, quotas, tariff barriers, import licenses, and so on became the rage. Quite naturally, international trade dwindled disastrously. Meanwhile bank after bank acquired foreign exchange as "assets." But how sound is a foreign exchange asset when international trade is suffocating under a system of controls and interventionism?

In 1931 the whole system came tumbling down, bank by bank, as the banks discovered that they were holding as reserves certain currencies, such as the dollar and the pound, which were subject to unpredictable devaluations. The devaluation of a reserve currency means the destruction of a portion of the central bank reserves of any country that uses that currency as a banking reserve. In turn that country must reduce its banking liabilities. The external devaluations lead to internal deflations. Great internal inflations had been

financed by the gold/exchange standard; the effect on foreign trade had been masked by administrative distortion of
foreign trade itself. Without the benefit of small continuous
adjustments, the system was allowed to build up explosive
pressures. Finally it succumbed.

During the 1930s the international monetary scene was
hardly to the sunny side of chaos. Exchange rates fluctuated
sometimes freely, sometimes under the influence of political
management. Nationalism was the prevailing passion. Competitive devaluations destroyed confidence and trade simultaneously. Phase Three was in terminal paralysis.

All the old wartime controls were instituted once again
during the Second World War. The money managers, however, looked ahead to the eventual return of peace, and were
concerned to design a system that would serve the free
world better than the now discredited gold/exchange standard.

That, in very sketchy terms, is the background of the conference of 1944 at Bretton Woods, where most of the central
bankers of the industrial world met to plan a system of monetary arrangements for the postwar period. What they came
up with was the IMF system, the system of the International
Monetary Fund and associated institutions. This is the
fourth and current phase of world monetary history; and
there is a rather good chance that it too is approaching
terminal paralysis. For there can be no question that the
repeated crises of Western key currencies in the past five or
six years are extremely harsh commentaries on the monetary
system that allows key currencies to approach the crisis
point time after time; that allows a key currency to remain
in payments imbalance for the better part of two decades;
that uses as a key currency one whose international convertibility into gold is de facto abolished.

In any event, the money managers at Bretton Woods were
convinced that whatever plan they came up with should
avoid what they considered to be the old pitfalls. The gold

standard was, in their view, as discredited as the gold/exchange standard, and it was axiomatic that any conference convening for the purpose of designing a system to facilitate world trade would repudiate at the outset the recent experiments with exchange controls, autarky, isolationism, and so on. They wanted stable exchange rates, general free convertibility among all developed currencies, and they wanted nothing to do with the gold standard. Their purpose was to promote international monetary cooperation, facilitate the expansion and growth of international trade, help exchange stability, assist in the establishment of a multilateral system of payments in respect to current transactions, and provide an opportunity to correct maladjustments in balance of payments without resorting to measures destructive of national or international prosperity.

So the IMF was set up. Each member country was required to contribute a "quota" that was computed on the basis of the country's monetary reserves, national income, volume of international trade, and so on. This quota determines not only the country's voting strength in deciding issues before the IMF, but it also defines the amount of assistance the country can claim from the IMF. Each member country pays its quota to the Fund in gold and its own currency—once again according to formula: gold to the extent of 25 per cent of the quota, or 10 per cent of the country's official reserves of gold *plus* dollars (U.S.), whichever is less. The remainder of the quota is paid in the national monetary unit, and the Fund's holdings of national currencies must be backed 100 per cent by a gold guarantee, in order to shield the Fund from losses through devaluation.

The Fund, then, forms a "pool" of currencies, and the member countries through their central banks (the Fund deals only with official institutions) enjoy "drawing" rights with the Fund. A country running a deficit against, say France, might settle the deficit by paying its own currency into the Fund and "drawing" in return a supply of French francs with which to make payment. The rate at which one currency is traded for another, the par value, is held constant within rather narrow limits.

Drawing rights are not unlimited. The IMF Articles do not allow a member to draw foreign exchange beyond the point where the Fund's holding of that member's currency equals 200 per cent of the member's quota. If the initial quota had been paid 100 per cent in gold, then the country's drawing right would be the currency equivalent of 200 per cent of its quota. If, as is the case, each quota was paid partly in the national currency, then each country's drawing right is reduced by that amount. Clearly, if the Fund's holdings of that country's currency have been reduced by other members' drawings of that currency, then the drawing right of the issuer is correspondingly increased.

There is a time limit also. Normally a country can draw 25 per cent of its quota without let or hindrance, but it cannot draw more than 25 per cent in any one year without subjecting itself to an examination by the Fund to see if the country is doing all it can to redress its deficit. Finally, the Fund tries to exercise some control over the use to which a country puts its drawings. In general the Fund seeks to help finance current trade deficits and refuses to cooperate in financing long-term capital investment or short-term currency speculation.

The Fund's facilities are not available for free. A charge of 0.5 per cent is assessed against drawings, and higher charges are made as the Fund's holdings of the drawer's currency exceed the quota. Repayment (i.e. the member buys its currency back from the Fund) is made according to a complicated formula; in no case does the Fund allow a drawing to be outstanding for more than five years, and most drawings are for far shorter periods.

The quotas were raised by 50 per cent in 1959 and again

by 25 per cent in 1965. Even at that the U.S. quota, for example, at about $4.5 billion, is hardly enough to finance one good deficit year.

The IMF Articles include other very important provisions, notably the specification of exchange rates. Every member is required to establish a par value for its currency either in relation to gold or in relation to the U.S. dollar. The dollar in turn is defined as $\frac{1}{35}$ ounce of gold, so that every member currency is directly or indirectly tied to gold. Naturally the day-to-day flow of supply and demand for a given currency will affect its exchange rate. Such fluctuations are permitted under the Articles to go to one per cent above or below par value—at which point the central bank is expected to intervene in the foreign exchange markets, either buying or selling reserves (gold or dollars) to maintain the exchange rate within limits.

Any alteration in exchange rates beyond an initial 10 per cent adjustment requires the agreement of the Fund, and the Fund will oppose any change in par value unless the country concerned can show there is a "fundamental disequilibrium" in the balance of trade—i.e. its currency is pegged too high or too low. No definition has ever been offered officially for "fundamental disequilibrium." It would be interesting to know whether the Fund would apply that phrase to the United States experience after 1950. In practice very few adjustments have been made. The system of par values has developed a pronounced stability, perhaps rigidity, at least among the major currencies, since 1950.

It is remarkable that the IMF system makes so little provision for the alteration of exchange rates. The United States is on its way towards twenty years of deficits, and yet there has been no suggestion of "fundamental disequilibrium." The normal explanation is that the dollar, because it is a reserve currency (other central banks count their dollar holdings as reserves), must be maintained at a given par with gold because if it were devalued it would cause immense losses throughout the world monetary system and bring in a wave of mistrust, disillusion, and protectionism.

Exchange rates are relatively fixed. The reserve currency cannot devalue. The Fund cannot finance long-term deficits in the reserve currency country. Yet it is obvious that the deficit country must sooner or later run out of reserves (gold) and credit (abroad) with which to finance its own deficit. What remains? The deficit country must deflate; or the surplus countries must inflate; or both. But that is exactly the medicine classically administered by the nineteenth-century gold standard.

No doubt because this basic flaw in the IMF design was so apparent, there have been steps to improve the ability of the international monetary system to respond to long-term imbalances in reserve currency countries. Besides the increases in quotas already mentioned, in 1952 the Fund introduced "stand-by credits" which guaranteed that certain sums would be available for certain periods. Countries enjoying these credits can treat them as part of their monetary reserves. In effect the credit standing of the Fund is transferred to the countries using the stand-bys. The credits have never exceeded about $2 billion.

Another and larger innovation was the General Agreements to Borrow—a protocol arranged in 1962 among ten members and the Fund, involving now $6 billion, and providing a huge source of funds to the Fund for the purpose of making loans to any country that has come under excessively heavy monetary pressure. In this arrangement the IMF merely serves as agent or intermediary (one thinks of the term made famous by Adam Clayton Powell Jr., "bag man"), but the size of the credit is such that it has been of major importance in resisting monetary "runs" like that against the pound sterling in 1964.

Even less directly related to the Fund's official operations is the London Gold Pool. Under this arrangement the same countries that entered into the General Agreements to

Borrow have formed a syndicate to buy and sell gold in London against whatever speculative trends may crop up. In effect any raid on London is thus spread out against ten potent central banks, and once the raid is over and gold is available again at a normal price, the Pool resumes acquisitions of gold, and its holdings are distributed to the members in accordance with a predetermined quota system.

One source of trouble for the Fund is its obvious subservience to London and Washington, a subservience that goes far to explain the low estate of the Fund's reputation in Europe. The English-speaking bloc plus a handful of economically associated countries control an absolute majority of the voting strength in the Fund. When, as has been the case in recent years, the principal activity of the Fund appears to have been emergency aid to the pound and the dollar, the non-Anglo-Saxon nations are certainly entitled to wonder why they should be forced, through higher Fund quotas, to contribute in this roundabout way to the perpetuation of what they consider to be faulty monetary policies in Washington and London. As of June 1965 the British accounted for 59.7 per cent of total net drawings from the Fund.

Sidney Rolfe has pointed out[1] that the present system has given rise to an unforeseen and not altogether happy supersystem. The IMF having failed to provide an adjustment mechanism for basic imbalances, there has developed an informal system of eclectic financing—the Group of Ten, the London Gold Pool, and some of the top officers of the IMF itself and the Bank for International Settlements (one need only think of the susurrous homilies issuing from Basle each year). This amounts to an international monetary Establishment, and like all Establishments it expects to have its way. Thus the international bankers who make loans to London to support the pound make demands, also, that London undertake basic reforms in order to resuscitate the pound over the longer term. In the last year the international mon-

etary fraternity have imposed upon Britain, even under a
socialist regime, the harshest and most austere economic policies seen in the West since the early days of German recovery. I do not dispute that the policies were correct. Nor
is it anything to wonder at that the bankers required such
policies as a sort of collateral for their loan. What is interesting is that the international monetary Establishment
has been able to dictate internal policy to a country osten-
sibly democratic. The central bankers of the West are fairly
independent of their own governments and they are really
remote from the voters of any country, including their own.
That they should be in a position to dictate internal policy
to foreign countries is a subject well worth thorough investigation. It is not, unfortunately, the main topic here.

Once again, though, one is entitled to ask whether this
result is so much superior to the old pure gold standard.
Under that system, the movements of gold reserves tended
to bring about deflations and inflations, in the direction
needed to reduce international price imbalances. That system is criticized on precisely that account. But the present
system has given rise to a new class of international monetary czars who dictate reforms just as harshly as gold might
have done, and who for their pains create a net increase in
international tension and hostility, not to mention their
effect on the operation of a democratic political system.

Jacques Rueff describes the foibles of the Fund with a
lovely simile:[2] "Thus administered, the Fund has all the
appearances of a system of convertibility, but it has none of
its regulatory virtues. It is like those wrist watches that the
very young wear. They have a dial, and hands that point,
but no works inside. The Bretton Woods institution permits
you to play at monetary convertibility without deriving the
benefits of it."

Another great French economist, Charles Rist, pointed out
in 1951 that the International Monetary Fund was not
working out well: "One can no longer conceal the fact that

the International Monetary Fund has clearly failed in its mission. Instead of bringing us closer to an international monetary standard (which was its true mission), it has organized a supranational monetary management based on maintaining paper moneys and proscribing gold. The futility of these efforts showed itself a few weeks ago when the gold-producing countries obtained permission to sell their production at a premium. Can one appeal to the Fund to obtain a reversal of its policy? I do not believe so. It is up to each country, therefore, to take the most efficient measures to protect itself against the occurrences of monetary crises."[3]

Prof. Harry G. Johnson of the University of Chicago has published some telling criticisms of the IMF: "The IMF was therefore designed to start the postwar world off with an international monetary system free of the defects of the previous system. But both defects in its design—particularly, the small size of the initial Fund and the erroneous basic assumption that all currencies can be treated as equal in international trade and payments—and the nature and magnitude of the immediate postwar monetary disequilibrium problem conspired to set the Fund outside the mainstream of developments . . . the emergence of the dollar as an international reserve currency has re-created the gold exchange standard of the 1920s, which broke down so disastrously in the 1930s with all its inherent problems. . . . The result has been that the present international monetary system has become a system of rigid exchange rates like the old gold standard, contrary to the intentions of the planners of the IMF; further contrary to the assumptions of the planners, it has proved impossible (or, at least, inexpedient) to devise effective controls over short-term capital movements, which have returned to plague the stability of the system . . . adjustment under the present system is a matter of *ad hoc* interventions in trade and payments designed to disguise disequilibrium, coupled with dependence on the passage of time in disequilibrium conditions to bring about genuine adjustment, contrary to the other policy objectives of the countries concerned. There is, indeed, a strong prevailing tendency to gloss over the difference between spurious and genuine adjustment, and in so doing to sanction the use of interventions in trade and payments to preserve the appearance of balance-of-payments equilibrium. To do so is to lose sight of the ultimate purposes of international monetary organization in the pursuit of a functioning international monetary system. The ultimate purpose of the international monetary system is to facilitate freedom of competition in trade and payments, and to free international transactions from arbitrary interventions prompted by monetary developments themselves. When freedom of international competition becomes subservient to the maintenance of a particular set of exchange rates, as it has increasingly done in recent years, means have changed places with ends."[4]

Sidney Rolfe concludes his analysis with much the same line of reasoning: "First, the balance-of-payment adjustment mechanism to eliminate imbalances is inefficient under the present system. . . . Second, world reserves and liquidity will not grow fast enough to finance future international payments imbalances. . . . Third, the first two deficiencies create a condition in which the international monetary system is inevitably prone to collapse. If the deficits of the reserve currency countries, especially the United States, should be permanently eliminated under the present system a shortage of world liquidity and reserves would soon develop. With inadequate world reserves, trade and investment would be retarded; a reversion to direct controls, competitive currency devaluations, and other beggar-thy-neighbor evils to accomplish balance-of-payments equilibrium would likely occur. But if, on the other hand, the deficit-reserve currency countries cannot stop their deficits, confidence in the continued convertibility between their currencies and gold will be lost, and runs on these currencies could force devaluation or crisis application of exchange restrictions, gold embargos, or other autarkic measures. The system seems damned if it does and damned if it does not. . . . While this brief diagnosis of the international financial system may be overdrawn, it does point up the logical contradictions which, if not mitigated, could result in severe disruption in international finance, trade, and capital flows."[5]

The case seems clear enough. The persistent deficits of the United States are causing profound concern in international monetary circles not only because American politicians are unwilling to take the domestic steps necessary to redress the balance but because the international monetary system is unequal to the twin task of disciplining the United States or sheltering itself from the ultimate and drastic collapse.

Notes

Chapter 3.
1. *Gold and World Power*, by Sidney Rolfe (New York: Harper, 1966), p. 102.
2. Rueff, op. cit., p. 62. Translation mine.
3. Charles Rist, *The Triumph of Gold*, tr. by Philip Cortney (New York: Philosophical Library, 1961), p. 177.
4. Harry G. Johnson, *The World Economy at the Crossroads* (Oxford: Clarendon Press, 1965), p. 20 ff.
5. Sidney Rolfe, op. cit., pp. 196–7.

A Look at the Banking System

> The reform measure finally enacted—the Federal Reserve System—with the aim of preventing any such panics or any such restriction of convertibility in the future [after the Panic of 1907] did not in fact stem the worst panic in American economic history and the severest restrictions of convertibility, the collapse of the banking system from 1930 to 1933 terminating in the banking holiday of March 1933. That same reform, intended to promote monetary stability, was followed by about thirty years of relatively greater instability in the money stock than any experienced in the pre-Federal Reserve period our data cover [1867 on], and possibly than any experienced in the whole of U.S. history, the Revolutionary War alone excepted.
>
> *A Monetary History of the United States 1867—1960,* by Milton Friedman and Anna Jacobson Schwartz (Princeton, 1963), p. 698.

THE problem of the balance of payments is of concern to American citizens because we shall all be affected by the outcome of the story. If Washington sets its policy by the precedent of the past, then it is only a matter of time before a financial storm from overseas engulfs us. If, instead, Washington follows the advice that foreign bankers and statesmen have offered for the past five or six years, an international storm will be headed off, but at the price of certain adjustments here at home. Our international payments position is greatly affected by our domestic monetary policy. In turn our domestic monetary policy may be viewed in terms of our management of the banking system. So, before going any further along the main route, it will be well to take a small detour by way of introducing the U.S. banking system in fairly simple terms.

If money is a medium of exchange, then its usefulness is enhanced if it is uniform. Thus exchanges will be free of the delay, expense, inconvenience, and risk of using a variety of coins and paper money circulating at different discounts or premiums.[1] For most of our history we have not had a uniform money. In colonial days the medium of exchange consisted mainly of paper bills of credit issued by the colonies and some foreign coins. Overissue of paper, depreciation, and default were common.

With the development of banking, about the beginning of the nineteenth century, notes issued by banks became the major part of our currency. Excepting the periods when the first Bank of the United States (1791 to 1811) and the second Bank of the United States (1816 to 1836) were in operation, most of our currency circulating before the War Between the States consisted of notes issued by state-chartered banks. Between 1811 and 1861 the number of state-chartered banks grew from less than 100 to approximately 1,600.

State bank notes were printed on all varieties of paper, they were of varying sizes, and they circulated at varying discounts. It is estimated that in 1861 the 1,600 banks chartered in 34 states were issuing about 10,000 different kinds of notes. Some were good and circulated at par, i.e. face value. Some were redeemable in coin at the issuing bank but circulated at a discount a few miles away because of transportation difficulties. Some, heavily overissued, circulated at a deep discount; some—many—became worthless. Because of the incomprehensible variety of notes, counterfeiters entered the picture, further complicating the stew. The War Between the States gave rise to "greenbacks" in the North and Confederate paper 'way down south in Dixie.

According to one estimate, the chaos in note issue and the innumerable bank failures brought about losses of about $100 million in face value of bank notes that became worthless. No wonder the state bank notes acquired such pejoratively humorous monickers as "wildcats" and "red dogs" and "stumptails."

Obviously something had to be done. A first step was the National Banking Act of 1863, which established uniform regulations for banks, required them to back their note issue with government bonds, limited their total issue to the amount of paid-in capital, and required them to maintain a redemption fund of lawful money in the Treasury. The result was a safe and uniform issue of national bank notes, but other forms of currencies still fogged the picture. In 1865 a law was passed placing a 10 per cent tax on state bank notes. They promptly expired. After 1865 all forms of currency were under federal control and regulation; and with the passage of the Gold Standard Act in 1900 the problem of uniformity was finally solved.

Another problem that cropped up early was the problem of redeemability of the currency. Banks would not have enough coin on hand to redeem the notes they had issued, or not enough cash (coin and national bank notes) to pay their depositors on demand. The problem arose first with bank notes, because their total volume exceeded the volume of bank deposits until the War Between the States. It was a twofold problem. First, the holders of the bank notes might encounter great difficulty in getting to the bank in question. Second, once they got there the bank might turn out not to have enough coin on hand. This situation in turn might come about because of the incompetence of the management (the banking business has its share of human disasters) or because of public panic. The panic followed a pattern: a period of expansion or speculation would invite some banks to overissue their notes. Those banks' solvency being called in question, the public would begin to suspect other banks, even the more prudently managed. A simultaneous demand that all banks redeem all their outstanding notes could be met only by the banks' closing their doors until things simmered down. Large amounts of coin could not be minted or transferred as fast as public rumor.

Before 1860 another form of money began to assume importance. Banks began making loans to their clients by crediting their deposit accounts rather than issuing notes to them. Such bank deposits, today's familiar checking account money, grew so fast that they were the principal form of money by the end of the century. Once again, however, there was the question of redeemability. Individual banks that had expanded their loans unwisely would find, in a pinch, that they didn't have enough cash (coin and national bank notes) to pay off their depositors. Other banks, prudently managed, would be hit by general panics over deposits just as they had been hit by general panics over bank notes. What was needed was a system of currency that could be expanded as needed whenever the public felt the desire for currency rather than deposits.

Some moves had already been made in this direction. In 1824 the Suffolk Bank of Boston agreed to redeem the notes of outlying banks, at par, if they would maintain balances with Suffolk for that purpose. The plan worked, and the notes of New England banks circulated generally at face value. In 1829 New York passed the Safety Fund Act requiring each bank to contribute to a fund that would guarantee the liabilities of banks that had failed—a precursor of the Federal Deposit Insurance Corporation. In 1838 New York passed the Free Banking Act, enabling banks to be chartered without special legislative approval if they met certain requirements, one of which was the deposit of certain securities with the comptroller to be sold if need be to redeem the bank's notes. New York also required banks to maintain a reserve in coin equal to at least 12.5 per cent of outstanding notes. This was one of the earliest of a long line of laws establishing reserves against the notes issued by private chartered banks. In 1842 Louisiana passed a law requiring banks to maintain a reserve (and quite a reserve: 33 1/3 per cent) against what it called "cash responsibilities" —a phrase that had the effect of including bank deposits as well as bank notes. The first specific mention of deposits requiring a reserve was in a Massachusetts law of 1858 requiring banks to maintain a reserve in specie equal to 15 per cent of the aggregate liability for notes *and* deposits.

Notes issued by country banks tended to accumulate in the cities through the normal course of trade. Country banks accordingly began keeping deposits in banks in key cities for the redemption of their notes. Banks in these "redemption cities" were soon holding substantial amounts of out-of-town bank balances. For the purpose of computing the legal reserve against note issue, only specie was originally considered. Now the country banks complained that they should also be allowed to count as their reserve their balances in redemption cities. Their complaints were heard, and before long the banking laws included the concept of redemption cities and the principle of counting as part of one bank's reserves its balances in other banks. In 1864 the National Banking Act of 1863 was vastly amended; it included the concepts of central reserve cities, reserve cities, and country banks, and it specified different reserve ratios for banks depending on their location. In the next 50 years some 40 states passed banking laws covering such items as reserve ratios, and the distinction between time deposits and demand deposits; but the periodic money panics continued: some, especially in the early years of this century, were among the worst this country had ever experienced. The Panic of 1907 was a classic. Benjamin Anderson tells it best: "Over the country generally in 1907 the clearing houses had provided emergency substitutes for cash in the form of clearing house checks, printed or engraved to look something like paper money, though usually on white paper—payable, not in cash, but 'through the clearing house,' endorsed by all the banks of the clearing house. This paper was accepted for local currency. Such currency was readily accepted far from home. In a typical Missouri town of 35,000 people in 1907 these clearing house checks or certificates were readily obtainable at the banks and were readily accepted by the local merchants. If, however, one needed to make a railroad trip, these certificates were not acceptable by the railroad for railroad tickets, nor were they readily acceptable by the merchants or others in a near-by city. The local banker understood this, and provided enough actual money for the purpose of making these trips. In this community, also, there was a great increase in the drawing of small checks, even as small as 25¢, in making local payments. . . . In New York City in 1907 the banks did not issue clearing house checks to circulate among the people. It was feared that New York currency would be 'too good' and would circulate too far from home. They paid out cash for necessary purposes, but restricted cash payments. They provided, for payments inside the clearing house, clearing house *loan certificates* 'good between the banks,' which they issued to individual banks, at 6% interest. In New York, however, important industrial companies issued printed checks for payroll purposes, usually in $5 denominations, which the merchants would accept. Thus the Standard Oil Company printed checks drawn on the National City Bank which it used for payroll purposes, and these had a very considerable circulation as actual currency with these two good names upon it. These checks were good through the clearing house. They would be received by any bank for deposit, and checks could be drawn against the deposits thus created. The deposit was kept mobile."[2]

In the wake of the spectacular Panic of 1907 there arose a demand for reform of the monetary system. In 1908 the

Congress appointed a National Monetary Commission to study the situation and make proposals. After several years of study the Commission returned its report and the Congress acted. On December 23, 1913, the Federal Reserve Act became law, establishing the Federal Reserve System. Senator Robert Owen, head of the Senate Committee on Banking and Currency, described the legislative purpose of the Act: ". . . to establish an auxiliary system of banking, upon principles well understood and approved by the banking community, in its broad essentials, and which, it is confidently believed, will tend to stabilize commerce and finance, to prevent future panics, and place the nation upon an era of enduring prosperity."[3]

It is worthy of note that the Federal Reserve System, through which the Federal Government acquired almost complete control of the nation's monetary arrangements, has failed to bring about the lofty results its creators hoped for. Instead of putting an end to panic, it presided over the worst depression in our history. Instead of beefing up the public confidence in the banking system, it stood by while the nation's banks closed their doors from coast to coast. Inflation and deflation, boom and bust, have been known even under the reign of the Federal Reserve System. Monetary stability, measured in terms of the long-term preservation of the purchasing power of the monetary unit, has been notably absent under the reign of the Federal Reserve System. Since 1913 the purchasing power of the dollar has declined by almost 75 per cent. It continues to decline, in total defiance of the pious hopes of Senator Owen.

There are more than 13,000 commercial banks in this country, and 6,130 of them are members of the Federal Reserve System. These "member banks" do about 85 per cent of the nation's banking business, however; so it is reasonable to consider the Federal Reserve System (the Federal Reserve Banks and the member banks together) as the long and the short of the nation's banking system.[4]

At the top of the operating pyramid is the Board of Governors of the Federal Reserve System (the Federal Reserve Board), situated in Washington, D.C. It consists of seven members, appointed for 14-year terms by the President with the advice and consent of the Senate. The Board issues regulations interpreting the laws relating to Federal Reserve Bank operations; it represents the Federal Reserve System in relations with the Federal Government; it exercises special supervision over the foreign contacts and international operations of the Federal Reserve Banks; it has full authority over reserve ratios (as a percentage of deposits) within limits set by the Congress; it establishes maximum rates of interest that member banks may pay on time (i.e. savings-type) deposits; it reviews and determines discount rates established by the Federal Reserve Banks; it directs the Federal Reserve System's activities in bank examinations and coordinates its economic research and publications; its approval is necessary in the appointment of the president and first vice-president of each Federal Reserve Bank (after their election by the board of directors of the Bank); and it appoints three of the nine directors at each Federal Reserve Bank, including the chairman and the deputy chairman.

The Federal Reserve Banks are corporations chartered by the Congress to operate in the public interest. There are twelve regional Federal Reserve Banks (with a total of 24 branches)—one for each Federal Reserve Region. The Federal Reserve Banks are at Boston, New York, Philadelphia, Cleveland, Richmond, Atlanta, Chicago, St. Louis, Minneapolis, Kansas City, Dallas, and San Francisco. The Federal Reserve System operates as a central bank, but clearly it is decentralized in some respects. The board of directors establishes the discount rate for each bank. The capital stock of the Federal Reserve Bank is owned by the member banks in its district. Earnings of the Federal Reserve Banks over and above a moderate return on the capital subscriptions of the member banks are handed over to the Treasury under the

rubric of interest on Federal Reserve Notes. The Federal
Reserve Banks hold the cash reserves of the member banks,
provide checking accounts to the Treasury, issue currency
(Federal Reserve Notes), collect checks, supervise and examine member banks, handle the issuance and redemption
of Government securities, and act as general fiscal agent for
the Federal Government.

The member banks, some 6,130 of them, include all of
the nationally chartered banks and most of the larger state-
chartered banks. The member banks elect six of the nine
directors on the policy-making board of their Federal Reserve Bank. Only three of these six may be bankers; the
other three must be actively engaged in commerce, industry,
or agriculture in the district, and may not be officers,
directors, or employees of any bank. (The third triad of
directors are appointed by the Federal Reserve Board and
must not be bankers or stockholders in any bank.) Member
banks must subscribe to the capital of their Federal Reserve
Bank to the tune of 6 per cent of their own capital and
surplus (half paid in, half subject to call); they must comply
with reserve requirements and with regulations governing
branch banking, check collection, and so on. In return they
have the right to borrow from the Federal Reserve Bank
when necessary; they can use Federal Reserve facilities for
collecting checks, settling balances, and transferring funds
to other cities; they can get currency (bills and coin) from
the Federal Reserve when needed; their capital contribution
to the Federal Reserve Bank earns 6 per cent a year.

The Federal Open Market Committee is a group of twelve
men (seven members of the Board of Governors and five of
the twelve Reserve Bank presidents) who decide on policy
for open market operations—i.e. the buying and selling of
securities in the open market. All open market transactions
are conducted for a single System Account by the Federal
Reserve Bank of New York in behalf of all the Reserve
Banks. These transactions are supervised by a Manager of

the System Account, who is an officer of the New York Federal Reserve Bank.

The Federal Advisory Council is a group of twelve citizens, each elected by the board of directors of a Federal Reserve Bank, usually from among the bankers of its district. The Council meets at least four times a year to confer with the Board of Governors on general business conditions and to make advisory recommendations on matters concerning the Federal Reserve System.

So much for the outward structure of the nation's banking system. Its functioning within that structure is what concerns us more closely. The primary objective of the Federal Reserve System is to keep the money supply in such relation to other aspects of the national economy that maximum stability will be achieved. The tools it uses in pursuing (vainly, I suspect) this objective are of two main types— 1) those that affect the use of credit for certain purposes and 2) those that affect the money supply and the reserve positions of banks.

I should pause to make clear that "money" these days is checking-account money more than anything else. The total money supply is about $170 billion, made up of about $39 billion of currency (bills and coin) and $131 billion of demand deposits (checking accounts) with the commercial banks. On this basis, checking-account money makes up about three-quarters of the money supply. Actually it is much more important than that figure might suggest. Checking-account money is used in something like 95 per cent of all transactions in this country.

The central characteristic of checking-account money is that it is an abstraction, not a tangible thing. You keep track of its quantity by making marks in books of account; that is all it is. Originally, as I mentioned earlier, you opened an account at a bank by taking your supply of coins and bills to the bank, depositing that hoard, and acquiring the right to "draw" against the bank. Eventually the banks facilitated the making of loans by simply extending the drawing right, i.e. "creating" a demand deposit in a checking account. If I go into your bank and borrow funds, I can write a check on your bank just as easily as you, who may have started up your account by depositing your pay envelope of bills and coins. My check-money is just as "real" as yours, and they can't be told apart in the marketplace. Money broadly conceived is anonymous debt: it represents the reasonable presumption that a payment in real goods and services will be made in the marketplace sometime in the future.

The member bank keeps its reserves at its Federal Reserve Bank. (Again, the language is metaphorical: the "reserve" is an accounting notation only.) Under the present system the commercial banks do not maintain a one-for-one ratio of reserves to deposit liabilities. The ratio is more like 20 per cent (it varies between country banks, reserve city banks, city banks; and the various ratios are variable). This means that the member bank can "create" $80 in checking-account money for every $20 it has as reserves with the Federal Reserve Bank.

Actually it wouldn't work quite that way. A schematized but more likely chain of events would be as follows. A man walks into Bank A with $100 in coins, deposits them, and opens a checking account in that amount. The bank counts the coins as part of its reserves. Supposing a reserve ratio set by the Federal Reserve Board at 20 per cent, Bank A will add $20 to its reserve account and have $80 of "excess reserves"—i.e. lendable funds. It makes additional loans of $80 in the form of demand deposits. Those customers spend their borrowed funds, paying $80 to customers of Bank B. Bank B receives $80 in deposits; it adds $16 (the 20 per cent reserve ratio again) to its reserve account and has $64 available for loans. It goes ahead and loans out the $64. Bank C, Bank D, and so on continue the chain, until at the theoretical end of the game exactly $400 in new loans (demand deposits, "money") has been created out of the air, "backed" by the $100 in coins the man originally brought to the bank. Conversely, a small withdrawal of cash from the banking system brings about a much larger loss of the system's money-creating power.

It is obvious, then, that under this system of "fractional reserve" banking any change in the total amount of bank reserves is capable of introducing vast changes in the money supply and perhaps correspondingly vast changes in the economic climate. What are the ways in which bank reserves can be altered?

There are three major ways: 1) gold movements, 2) an increase or decrease in the currency circulating, and 3) the lending activities (including "open market operations") of the Federal Reserve System.

The Treasury adds to the supply of bank reserves when it purchases newly mined or imported gold. In payment for the gold the Treasury draws a check on the Federal Reserve and usually restores its deposit by issuing a gold certificate to the Federal Reserve. When this check is deposited by the gold-seller some bank receives an increase in deposits, and its reserve is correspondingly increased.

Since the banks' holdings of currency are counted as part of their reserves, any increased preference for currency in the hands of the public will tend to reduce the bank reserves (this is the mechanism of all "runs" on the bank). If the public returns the bills and coin to the banking system and tends to do more by check, the banking reserves will be increased. The rise and fall of public preference for currency is offset by Federal Reserve loans of abstract reserves to the member banks to compensate for their loss of "real" reserves in the form of bills and coin.

Until 1965 it used to be that the gold certificate account of the Federal Reserve System was used as "backing" for the aggregate amount of Federal Reserve Notes and deposit liabilities. The law required the gold backing to be at least 25 per cent of the combined notes and liabilities. By early

1965 the reserve ratio was down to 27.5 per cent and at the current rate of decline it would have hit bottom in about a year. Chairman Martin of the Federal Reserve Board reported to the Congress in early February 1965 that he favored the President's proposal that the gold reserve requirement be removed from Reserve Bank deposit liabilities but that it be kept as backing for Federal Reserve Notes: ". . . by retaining the traditional gold 'backing' for Federal Reserve notes, the proposal would be reassuring to those who, in their continuing concern for the stability of the dollar, see in a gold cover requirement an important element of strength. The value of any currency is so much a product of confidence that one should not disregard this advantage of S. 797."[5]

Two years later the Administration was talking of removing the gold backing from the Federal Reserve Note issue—in order, as it explained, to provide maximum gold availability for international settlements. So it seems reasonable to suppose that gold movements, in the future, will not bear any formal relation to the domestic money supply.

That leaves two ways for bank reserves to change in volume: they may change as the public desire for hand-to-hand currency expands or contracts; they may change in accordance with the lending policies of the Federal Reserve. The Federal Reserve has next to zero control over the public preference for cold cash, which is a highly seasonal and occasionally emotional thing. The Federal Reserve's control over the money supply is limited, then, to its lending operations and its operations in the credit markets—specifically, its control over the reserve ratio, its discount rate, and its open market operations.

Member banks may replenish their reserves in the Federal Reserve Banks either by discounting some of their customers' notes or by borrowing on their own notes, using Government securities or other satisfactory assets as collateral. In either case, the proceeds are credited to the member banks, increasing their reserves. The rate of interest charged for these extensions of credit by the Federal Reserve Banks is called the discount rate. By raising or lowering the discount rate the Federal Reserve Banks can make it more or less expensive for member banks to get additional reserves through the Federal Reserve credit facilities.

Such changes affect the general credit situation in a number of ways. Directly: changing the discount rate alters the cost of getting additional reserves from this source. Indirectly: there is a marked tendency for corresponding changes to appear in the rates that member banks charge their customers in turn, especially for short-term loans in money-market centers. Changes in the discount rate are of importance also as a sign of a change in Federal Reserve Board attitude towards the economy in general as well as the credit market in particular.

Another instrument of the Federal Reserve Board is its authority to alter the legal reserve ratio. This is the proportion (expressed in percentage) of net demand deposits that must be held as a reserve with the Federal Reserve Banks. (Net demand deposits are total demand deposits minus cash items in process of collection [float] and also minus demand balances due from domestic banks.) As of early 1967, for example, the Federal Reserve Board had established reserve requirements of 16.5 per cent for reserve city banks, 12 per cent for country banks, 4 per cent for time deposits, and 4 or 5 per cent (depending on the amount of deposits) for other time deposits. The Board's authority operates only within limits established by the Congress; in recent years the reserve ratios established by the Board have been bumping along near the lower limits (i.e. near the most expansionary or inflationary limits) available under the law. This instrument has no direct effect on bank reserves; instead, it affects the amount of deposits that can be supported by a given amount of reserves. An increase in the reserve ratio tends to limit member bank loans and investments, and a decrease tends to encourage them. The reserve ratio alone is not necessarily adequate to effect a change in money-market conditions: if, while raising the reserve ratio (a stringency), the Federal Reserve Board lowers the discount rate (an easing), the reserves that the member banks might lose through higher reserve requirements might be borrowed back from the Federal Reserve at harmless interest cost. There is also the possibility that nothing at all will come of a change in the reserve ratio. As happened during the 1930s, the banks may simply keep their excess funds idle, perhaps because there are no opportunities for investment— a circumstance, in turn, that might come about when the entrepreneurs of the land have lost confidence or are deprived of incentive or are under the sway of pessimistic theorcticians (as in the 1930s, when academic observers on loan to Washington declared that the U.S. economy was "mature" and had no need of further investment).

Finally, the Federal Reserve may influence the volume of reserves in commercial banks by buying or selling securities and "eligible paper" (money market instruments acceptable for this purpose) directly in the open market. Most of such transactions involve U. S. Government securities, although the Federal Reserve is authorized to deal also in such paper as bankers' acceptances and bills of exchange.

Open-market purchases by the Federal Reserve tend to build up bank reserves. When the Federal Reserve buys securities from dealers, the dealers receive in payment checks drawn on the Reserve bank. When the dealers deposit these checks, the total deposits in commercial banks are increased. When the banks send these checks to the Federal Reserve for collection, the Federal Reserve credits their reserve accounts. The result of an open-market purchase by the Federal Reserve, then, is increases in commercial bank deposits and commercial bank reserves.

Because the Federal Reserve System concentrates its open-market operations in New York City through the System Account handled by the Federal Reserve Bank of New York, the initial impact of open-market operations is felt in the New York market. Depending on economic and investment conditions, Federal Reserve purchases in the open market may result in banks' increasing their commercial loans or instead using their new-found reserves to reduce their outstanding indebtedness to the Federal Reserve.

Federal Reserve operations in the open market have an effect, also, on the level of interest rates in general. System purchases of Government securities tend to bid up their price and lower their yield.* Treasury obligations being now the major segment of the money market, a lower yield on them tends to lower the yield on private obligations. Also, excess reserves may cause member banks, especially in the money-market centers, to lower their interest rates as a means of encouraging borrowing so that they may put their idle funds to work. Any change in the pattern of interest rates will influence the investment policies of all financial institutions. Open-market operations have been used to supplement the discount rate. When member banks have excess reserves and the Federal Reserve would like to apply higher interest rates, System sales in the open market in sufficient quantity may absorb so much of the members' reserves that they are forced to resort to borrowing from the Reserve Banks, thus making the discount rate effective.

The Federal Reserve Board also has control over the credit conditions in the organized stock markets—it can set the so-called "margin" requirements, the maximum amount an investor may borrow against his securities. This power has been wielded rather haphazardly and without really visible results. Indeed, there is ground to question whether it amounts to any "control" of the amount of credit in the

---

* Yield is the rate of return on investment, calculated as earnings as percentage of capital invested. Bond earnings (interest) are at a fixed number of dollars per year; bond prices vary according to supply and demand. Thus the inverse relation: larger the price, smaller the yield.

stock exchanges anyway. Funds obtained by borrowing against one kind of asset may be used to acquire another; is that other asset "wholly owned" or is there a potential claim on it? In 1929 there was hardly such a thing as consumer debt, instalment purchasing, or other forms of credit now widely extended and in huge amounts in this country, but there was a great deal of borrowed money at work in the stock market. Today there *appears* to be less credit in the stock market, while the amount of individual borrowing in other markets (retail, real estate, personal, etc.) has grown tremendously. In 1929 a stock market crash could trigger a collapse in real estate. Today a collapse in real estate could trigger a stock market crash.

The next chapter will have something to say about our present monetary situation and the role played by inflation in bringing about financial chaos.

Notes

Chapter 4.

1. The historical sketch is taken—in some places, bodily—from *The Quest for Stability*, a pamphlet issued in 1954 by the Federal Reserve Bank of Philadelphia. The material is in the public domain, and by and large in the public interest.

2. Benjamin M. Anderson, *Economics and the Public Welfare: Financial and Economic History of the United States, 1914–1946* (New York: D. Van Nostrand, 1949). A glorious book, and one that eminently deserves being reissued.

3. Quoted in *The Quest for Stability*, supra, p. 10.

4. Banking statistics are available in any *Federal Reserve Bulletin*.

5. Quoted in *Federal Reserve Bulletin*, February 1965, p. 228.

★ ★ ★ ★ ★ ★ ★

Chapter Five

★ ★ ★ ★ ★ ★ ★

Inflation Managers or Money Managers?

In the past year serious study has been undertaken of the functioning of the international monetary system and the possible needs for increased liquidity. While it is difficult to anticipate the longer-term evolution of the system, recent experience has highlighted two important points: one is that cooperation among the monetary authorities can contribute substantially to maintaining orderly conditions on the exchange markets; the other is that the disturbances that arise from inflation cannot be resolved by illusions about liquidity creation but only by acting on inflation itself.

> Gabriel Ferras
> General Manager
> Bank for International Settlements
> Annual Report, 1964

"Tell me again. How does the Federal Reserve regulate credit?"
John F. Kennedy to a staff aide during the 1960 campaign[1]

STRANGE to say, there is no such thing as a generally accepted definition of "money." Or to speak more precisely: no definition of money is very helpful in the real world. Take money as a medium of exchange—for that is the commonest definition and the most inclusive—and then face the problem of calculating how much money there is in, say, the

United States. (Some texts consider as additional functions or definitions of money the store of value, means of deferred payment, standard of value; but Ludwig von Mises points out that these are merely special cases of the medium of exchange). The difficulty is that the medium of exchange is what you and I think it is. I may have stashed away $100 in a savings account for the explicit purpose of earning a bit of interest between now and next Christmas, at which time I intend to convert my savings funds into a medium of exchange. Savings accounts are ordinarily excluded from the stock of money "narrowly defined."

A corporate financial officer may discover that the company has several thousand dollars on hand that won't be needed until tax time, or the annual inventory buildup. He may buy a certain kind of interest-bearing security issued by commercial banks (the certificate of deposit). In recent years the amount of money tied up in these CDs has climbed to dozens of billions—and yet the common notion of money excludes the CD.

The conventional definition of money is: checking account deposits, plus paper and coins. In the light of vastly increased holdings of interest-bearing forms of deferred exchange potential, more and more students of money are coming to think of the stock of money as the sum of checking deposits, paper and coins, time and savings deposits, savings and loan shares, savings bonds, and U.S. Government obligations due within one year (another favorite haven for temporarily excess corporate funds). Milton Friedman in A Monetary History of the United States uses the ampler definition but excludes short-term U.S. Government obligations.[2] Probably the "true" or "theoretical" quantity of money is no less than the Friedman figure and no more than the "broadly conceived" figure which is arrived at by including the sum of short-term government paper (i.e. bills and notes).

The question is not simply abstract fretting. It is of central

importance to the great, the perennial problem of inflation.
If inflation can be shown to be unrelated to the total stock
of money, then the problem of calculating the money stock
is irrelevant. The classical theory, called the Quantity
Theory, holds that increases in the money stock tend to introduce increases in the price level. For this theory it is proper to think of inflation as any increase in the money stock,
and an increase in the price level as exactly that, an increase in the price level.

Two recent government publications show to what lengths
our official warders will go to avoid such nomenclature. In
1966 the Board of Governors of the Federal Reserve System
published a monograph by Glenn H. Miller Jr. entitled *The
Process of Inflation: A Review of the Literature and Some
Comparisons of Cyclical Performance, 1953–1965.* The
Quantity Theory is given barely one sentence, on page 4;
Friedman and his *Monetary History* are not mentioned, and
this in an essay of some 60,000 words and capped with a
presumably extensive bibliography; though Friedman had
been off the presses for two years when Miller was writing;
and had scandalized the profession—because his immense
labors tended to produce statistical confirmation of the
Quantity Theory.

Again: in 1951 the Federal Reserve Bank of New York
published a small pamphlet, first edition, entitled "A Day's
Work at the Federal Reserve Bank of New York." Something
extremely interesting appears on page 22 thereof. Says the
New York Fed: "There is still another and more important
element of public interest in the operation of banks beside
the safekeeping of money: banks can 'create' money. One of
the most important factors to remember in this connection is
that the supply of money affects the general level of prices—
the cost of living." Accompanying this passage the Fed
published a graph that correlated the money stock and the
Cost of Living Index from 1941 to 1950—and sure enough
the two lines of the graph run along like the Dioscuri.

This, of course, was heresy. In the second edition of "A Day's Work," published in May 1953, the hand of the censor was evident. The analogous passage appears on page 20 and reads as follows: "There is still another and more important element of public interest in banking: banks can 'create' money. They can't do it without cost or risk, however, because the process of creating money involves checking on loans, handling deposits, and taking the chance of not being paid. One of the most important factors to remember about banks' creating money is that the supply of money affects not only the price level but also our daily decisions to spend or save." The graph showing a correlation between the money stock and the price level is omitted from the 1953 (and all later) editions.

Back in 1953 the ideological censorship exercised by the Federal Reserve Bank of New York might be understood as mere prejudice. Mr. Miller's delinquency in 1966 is a scandal, because he had available to him the revolutionary findings of Friedman and Schwartz and he refused even to acknowledge them. Friedman and Schwartz, summing up on page 676, write: "Throughout the near-century examined in detail we have found that: 1) Changes in the behavior of the money stock have been closely associated with changes in economic activity, money income, and prices. . . ." And they go on to recount that in the past century there had been two "major" eras of rising prices—1914 to 1920, and 1939 to 1948. In both eras there was "also a more than doubling in the money stock." Friedman and Schwartz found four periods of "relatively high degree of economic stability" (1882–1892, 1903–1913, 1923–1929, 1948–1960). Each of the four periods also showed "a high degree of stability in the year-to-year change in the stock of money." After giving more examples of economic cycles and their connection with monetary events, they conclude: "Of relationships revealed by our evidence, the closest are between, on the one hand, secular and cyclical movements in the stock of money and,

on the other, corresponding movements in money income
and prices."

The Quantity Theory holds, among other things, that the
price level will be steady if the money stock keeps pace
with the growth of industrial production. Recently the
American Institute of Economic Research published some
figures that show just such a correlation (or at the very least,
suggestive coincidence) for almost two dozen countries,
covering a period from 1950 to 1965[3]:

	Average Annual Increase (in %)		
	of Purchasing Media	of Industrial Production	of the Cost of Living
Venezuela	8	9	1.3
West Germany	10	9	1.6
Switzerland	6	4*	1.8
Belgium	5	4	2.0
Canada	6	6	2.2
Philippines	7	10	2.2
Portugal*	7	8	2.3
Italy	9	9	3.4
Netherlands	6	6	3.8
United Kingdom	3	3	3.8
Sweden	7	4	4.1
Japan	15	16	4.1
Denmark	6	6	4.2
Norway	5	5	4.4
France	12	6	5.5
Austria	10	7	5.5
Mexico	13	7	5.7
Spain	13	10	6.8
Argentina	22	2	28.3
Brazil	39	9	31.8

*Partial data.

The weaknesses in the data must be granted. Industrial
production indices can be far off. Every cost-of-living index

is a statistical abstraction that partakes deeply of the pre-judices of its authors. One country's concept of purchasing media may differ profoundly from another's (the old prob-lem of the proper definition of money). But the grossest evaluation of the figures given above must suggest a similar-ity in the orders of magnitude of 1) the degree to which the money stock grows faster than the supply of real goods and 2) the degree of growth in the price level.

This is all that is meant, really, when an observer remarks that there is an "inflation" (growth in the money supply) that may be the precursor of a general rise in the price level; and that concern is relevant in the context of the balance of payments, because world trade certainly does not favor the country that prices itself out of the market.

This is why it is so important for any student of interna-tional payments problems to take a good look at the domestic monetary policies of the countries he has under the scope. The record of recent years makes somber reading. Since 1945 the amount of mortage debt outstanding in the U.S. has grown from $35.5 billion to $366 billion. In the same period the amount of mortgage loans held by commercial banks (i.e. the amount of real estate credit extended by them) went from $4.8 billion to $54.7 billion. Consumer credit has risen from $5.7 billion to $92.5 billion. Instalment credit has risen from $2.5 billion to $73.6 billion. Commercial banks have eagerly waded into the flowing stream of instalment credit, lifting their loans in this line from a mere $745 million in 1945 to $32 billion by the first quarter of 1967.

Since 1945 the total gross debt of the U.S. Government has risen from $279 billion to $332 billion. The federal defi-cit in the current fiscal year may touch $30 billion, a new record. (A federal deficit does not necessarily mean inflation. If it is financed by genuine borrowing and not by the crea-tion of new bank deposits, then by definition—or at least by my definition—it is not inflationary.) The huge new federal deficits of recent years have not been financed by genuine borrowing. Instead, they have been financed largely by indirect taxation (federal agencies and trust funds raised their holdings of federal debt instruments from $27 billion to $70 billion) and by sales of about $20 billion in paper to the Federal Reserve Banks (their holdings have climbed from $24.3 billion to $44 billion).

Marcus Nadler says: "Borrowing by the Treasury from the Reserve Banks not only creates new purchasing power for the Treasury but also reserves for the member banks. The Treasury spends the acquired deposit at the Reserve Banks and the recipients of the checks deposit them with the member banks, increasing deposits and reserves by the same amount. Since only a part of the gained reserves (16–20 per cent) is needed as legal reserves against the deposits, the resulting excess reserves can be used as a basis for multiple credit expansion. Borrowing from the central banks (all other relevant factors remaining unchanged) is thus highly inflationary."[3]

This is the famous process known as "monetizing the debt." Since it is the business of bankers to put their reserves to work, you might expect the expansion of the money stock to be on the order of magnitude of the amount of debt monetized, multiplied by the deposit ratio. The $20 billion of federal debt swallowed by the Reserve Banks, multiplied by a deposit ratio of about 6, yields $120 billion—which is just about the amount of expansion in the deposit component of the money stock these past two decades. If the money stock has increased by almost doubling, any adherent of the Quantity Theory would expect the price level to go up proportionately. Since 1945 the Consumer Price Index has risen from 62.7 (letting 1957–1959 equal 100) to approximately 120. Since 1945, then, the dollar has lost approximately half of its purchasing power.

Debt is not good or bad in itself. Like a federal deficit, it may or it may not have bad effects. The thing to look for when there's a federal deficit is how it is financed. When the private sector piles up huge deficits we should ask the same question. Now all of this enormous private debt (for mortgages, instalment credit, consumer credit, and so on) is financed by an equally enormous accumulation of private savings. Mutual savings banks and savings and loan associations (the latter almost unknown in 1940) have picked up about $150 billion in deposits since 1945. Commercial banks have picked up almost the same amount of time deposits. It is these deposits which have financed the vast explosion of consumer debt, but simply to have a dollar of deposits in the banking system for every dollar the consumers owe to the banks is not enough to have a healthy banking system. There is the crucial matter of *timing*. It is common knowledge that an interest-bearing deposit in a bank can be withdrawn by the depositor on rather short notice—thirty days, usually; in some cases ninety. It is equally common knowledge that bank loans to consumers are on much longer terms: the mortgage may run thirty years, the auto loan three years, an industrial loan five years. So it should also be common knowledge that the banking system as a whole is in a most uncomfortable position. It has borrowed something like $300 billion and has promised to pay it back on short notice. It has loaned that $300 billion out on long-term loans. What would happen if, suddenly, only a small portion of the depositors asked the banks to make good? More than one observer stays awake nights on that one.

As a matter of fact, around mid-1967 there was talk that the monetary authorities were thinking of requiring depositors in savings institutions to give substantial advance notice before they could withdraw their funds; if the talk was accurate, it amounted to official recognition of the non-liquidity of the savings industry.

Some observers display only minimal concern in this connection, arguing that the people who owe the debts are the same ones who own the savings accounts; that it is a "wash" situation. Not so, says George Katona, head of the Survey

Research Center of the University of Michigan. Fully one-half of the country's families have less than $1,000 in savings and only 16 per cent of the families have more than $10,000 in savings. "Most of the persons in debt," says Katona, "have little savings; savings in this country continue to be highly concentrated."[5]

And that is just the trouble. Consumers who have loaded themselves with debts are finding it more and more difficult to service their debts.[6] The American Bankers Association took a survey of debt delinquency and found that in April 1967 consumers were 30 days or more behind in their debt payments on 1.75 per cent of all instalment bank loans—the highest delinquency rate since the low point of the 1960–1961 recession, and substantially up from the 1.64 per cent rate of April 1966. The actual figures on consumer debt are not without point:

	Average Family Income	Average Debt Service	Debt Service as Per Cent of Income
1966	$8,300	$1,833	22.0%
1965	7,780	1,690	21.7
1964	7,325	1,553	21.2
1961	6,220	1,223	19.6
1958	5,670	1,044	18.4
1955	5,090	870	17.0
1952	4,570	679	14.8
1949	3,860	441	11.4

Some were actually proud of this gigantic creation of debt. Said Mr. Herbert P. Patterson, executive vice president of the Chase Manhattan Bank, in a speech delivered in July 1966: "Let's look at the positive developments that have taken place in commercial banking in recent years. For one thing, banks have managed to increase their relative share of the total credit markets appreciably. Between 1955 and

1960, they handled about 18% of the total financing in the economy; between 1960 and 1965, their share increased to 35%. . . . This move ahead has been fueled largely by term loans to corporate customers, by real estate lending, instalment lending, by foreign lending and by new forms of credit extension. Aggressive lending policies have been possible because banks have been able to tap vast new sources of loanable funds—for instance, negotiable CDs, Euro-dollars,* savings deposits and savings certificates . . . banking is an ultra-modern business with a brilliant future . . . it is a booming business . . . a business on the move . . . a business that today is putting more money to work more profitably than ever before."[7]

As things turned out, the date of Mr. Patterson's speech would have been a good time to sell bank stocks short.

For it was the moment of the great credit stringency. After two decades of frantic finance, the nation's banking system came to the bottom of the barrel in the summer of 1966. The Magic Fives, long-term U.S. bonds originally issued at the astounding price of 5%, were selling at a sick discount. Triple-A corporate bonds, such as the issues of American Telephone & Telegraph, were selling to yield almost 6% and Double-A corporates were bringing more than 6% even with five-year call protection. Bank stocks were down 14% from a year before. Between 1955 and 1965 the commercial banks had extended as much credit as they had extended in the entire 41 years from the founding of the Federal Reserve System in 1914 to the beginning of the Debt Decade in 1955. The Federal Reserve System, having presided over the entire affair, decided to blow the whistle in the summer of 1966. It embarked on a program of reducing the availability of credit to the member banks. The member banks felt an

* Surplus dollar balances held in European institutions, redeemable in gold but at Washington's displeasure, and traded around among European institutions at a price (interest rate) that reflects the desirability or undesirability of the dollar as an international trading medium.

intensification of a pinch that had set in a year earlier, as testified by their presentation of "eligible paper" to the Federal Reserve System for discount (normally a bank will deposit federal obligations with the Federal Reserve and borrow against them in order to increase its reserves and hence its loaning capacity; when it has run out of federal paper, it can present commercial paper, "eligible" but at a half-point penalty):

Eligible Paper Presented by Member Banks
as Collateral for Borrowing at Federal Reserve Banks[8]

	No. of Pieces	Face Amount (billions)	No. of Banks
1966	24,345	$20.1	82
1965	18,343	7.2	40
1964	841	.2	20
1963	277	.1	8

Simultaneously the Federal Deposit Insurance Corporation issued warnings to non-member banks that they should "watch their liquidity"[9] because it appeared that savings flows into banks were significantly below the year-ago figure even though bank lending to business was up 20 per cent.

And why might that be? Because the Money Managers had decided to reorganize the savings market, that's why. The Federal Reserve Board, the Federal Home Loan Bank Board, and the Federal Deposit Insurance Corporation, which wield just about total control over the time deposit business, "adjusted" the various "ceilings" on interest rates on time deposits in September 1966—with the usual bureaucratic madness. There was established a "ceiling" of 4 per cent interest on "regular" savings accounts of commercial banks—5 per cent on other types of time deposits—5.5 per cent if you were an old established depositor—even more if you deposited $100,000 or more—or 5 per cent in a mutual savings bank—or 4.75 per cent at a Savings & Loan—unless you live in California, Hawaii, or Alaska, where you get 5.25 per cent—or up to 5.75 per cent with a certificate account, depending on where you live.

Let a hundred interest rates bloom! How unlovely is the bureaucratic mind. Why discriminate against Hawaii? Why discriminate in favor of California or Nevada? Why discriminate against small savers? Why discriminate against commercial banks?

There has never been a logical explanation of the hodge-podge interest rate structure designed by the Money Managers. All we know is that all Hell broke loose as a result of their indiscriminate tinkering. It all goes back to the Federal Reserve's desire to help the commercial banks increase their deposits. A new form of deposit, the CD, was introduced, through which the commercial banks offered interest rates of 5 per cent or more on funds guaranteed to be left on deposit for a year or so. As should have been foreseen, huge sums were sucked out of lower-yielding temporary investments such as "regular" savings accounts, Savings & Loan associations, and so on. A rate war commenced. The Savings and Loans were soon offering 5.5 per cent themselves—a dangerous tactic, because they were in no position to increase their earnings from their mortgage portfolios, which had been put out at significantly lower interest rates over the years. In response to construction industry demand for protection from the forces of the market, the savings industry actively sponsored the legislation that was put in force in September 1966.

Barron's (Sept. 26, 1966) commented: "Just when Congress, presumably in an effort to restrain inflation, has moved to curb industry's incentives to expand, the new rules seek to stimulate home finance and housing, perhaps the most dangerously inflated economic areas of all. Ten days before the annual meeting of the International Monetary Fund, where the dollar again will come under hard-eyed scrutiny, the U.S., by seeking to lower interest rates, has given its foreign creditors fresh cause for mistrust."

Dr. Roy L. Reierson, economist for Bankers Trust Company, commented: "The monetary authorities, by holding the ceiling rate on time deposits below the market, have adopted the novel technique of impeding the ability of the commercial banks to attract or even to retain their deposit volume. . . . As these pressures intensify, the risk increases that the impact on the economy may turn out to be more drastic than warranted or intended."[10]

Meanwhile there were two interest rates that remained unchanged. Large CDs and the Federal Reserve discount rate remained the same. Close observers did not overlook this event, and reasoned that the Federal Reserve was trying to acquire even tighter control of the major banks. The scheme was to adjust interest rates so that a huge runoff of funds would occur out of CDs and into other forms of short-term investment outside the commercial banking system. This would force the banks to sell their remaining government securities and eligible paper and finally borrow from the Federal Reserve more heavily than usual. Such borrowing would entitle the Federal Reserve to exercise much closer control over the type and purpose of the loans the banks would propose to make with the funds newly borrowed from the Federal Reserve.

Lee Silberman, writing in the *Wall Street Journal* (October 5, 1966), gave voice to the rising concern: "Is the Federal Reserve System edging dangerously toward a program of direct wire-pulling to guide the actions of the nation's private banking system? . . . Up until now, the Federal Reserve and the private banking community have operated as a partnership, the Fed setting the general framework of credit availability and cost, and the banks allocating resources within that framework. Now with one of the partners determined to meddle in the allocation process as well, the relationship is almost certain to undergo severe strains. The entire encounter raises questions about the nation's banking and credit institutions not only in this present period of stress but for future years as well."

It would appear, then, that the Federal Reserve System has wielded a great deal of power over the banking industry and is reaching out for even greater power (with nary a question of the legality of its aggression), that the banking system is highly distorted through its enormous propensity to borrow short and lend long, that even a minor shakeout such as occurred in 1966 is enough to send nervous shudders from coast to coast, that the Money Managers have stopped even attempting to manage the money supply and are dedicated to a policy of inflation-for-inflation's-sake, and that the blame for the final collapse of the system must be placed where it belongs: in the laps of the Money Managers.

From the standpoint of the international monetary situation, the unending American inflation is a genuine threat. The present international system is dedicated to maintaining a fixed exchange rate among the leading currencies—that is, no matter how deep the dollar falls as a consequence of perennial inflation, it is "supposed" always to be equal to a fixed number of marks or francs or guilders. The prevailing myth has two heads: 1) that inflation (increase in the money stock) has nothing to do with the price level, and 2) that the price level has nothing to do with a nation's international trading position. There are even those who say a nation's international trading position has nothing to do with its payments position, its payments position is independent of its gold flow, and the gold flow has nothing to do with the soundness of its money. For such as these, perpetual inflation is the breath of life. Wonder what they'll have to say when they get the breath knocked out of them?

Notes

Chapter 5.
1. Quoted in *Wall Street Journal*, Dec. 5, 1966. [I.e. six years late.]
2. *A Monetary History of the United States 1867–1960*, by Milton Friedman and Anna Jacobson Schwartz (Princeton, 1963), p. 4.
3. Economic Education Bulletin, *Paper Gold*, March 1967: American Institute for Economic Research, Great Barrington, Massachusetts.
4. *The Money Market and Its Institutions*, by Marcus Nadler et al. (New York: Ronald, 1955), p. 195.
5. *Wall Street Journal*, May 31, 1967.
6. Consumer debt figures from *ibid*.
7. Quoted in *Barron's*, 29 August 1966.
8. *Monetary Report*, by Alden R. Wells, May 1967, Issue No. XXXIII.
9. As reported in the *New York Times*, 19 September 1966.
10. Quoted in *Barron's*, 26 September 1966.

★ ★ ★ ★ ★ ★ ★

Chapter Six

★ ★ ★ ★ ★ ★ ★

The Only International Money

INTERNATIONAL trade gives rise to international payments, and it will be the task of this chapter to describe how international payments are consummated.[1]

If all trade were conducted on the shoulders of only one currency, then there would be no trouble in making payments across international borders. All transactions would "wash" in the one currency. Of course that is not the case. World trade is conducted in the multitude of the world's currencies. An American tobacco exporter may sell in Britain for sterling. A British importer may need dollars in order to pay for American automobiles. Besides commercial trade there are many other transactions that lead to a desire to exchange one currency for another, to acquire "exchange." Americans might need foreign exchange in order to finance direct investments overseas. The same need arises when Americans, say, purchase foreign long-term securities or short-term money-market instruments. American tourists heading overseas will need to acquire foreign currencies—at a current rate of a couple of billion dollars' worth per year. American troops stationed overseas create a need for the purchase of foreign currencies.

It would be extremely difficult to consummate the infinite number of international transactions if each transaction had to be arranged as a special problem in foreign exchange—if, say, our American exporter of tobacco refuses to go through with the deal until he has lined up an American importer who needs the sterling that the tobacco exporter is about to acquire. The large number of individual transactions, the incredible variety of payments methods, the individual variations in the purchasing power of the various currencies— all of these factors, and others too, have justified the development of a special market which devotes itself to the buying and selling of foreign exchange.

Changing dollars into foreign exchange or foreign exchange into dollars is normally the function of commercial banks, since the great bulk of transactions whether international or national are "settled" through the alteration of checking account balances in commercial banks. Most of the great commercial banks are able to handle their own foreign exchange requirements much of the time, but there is obviously going to be a net shortage or surplus of this currency or that, and it is the work of the foreign exchange market to translate those imbalances into changes in the "price" of foreign currencies vis-a-vis each other—changes in the "exchange rate."

The center of the foreign exchange market in the U.S. is New York City. It is not a physical market like the Stock Exchange or the Commodity Exchange. It doesn't run on regular hours, say 9 to 5. It has no rules or regulations other than the unwritten code that has evolved over the centuries. It is a mechanism, an institution, which helps buyers and sellers of foreign exchange to get in touch and arrange transactions. Almost all of the "getting in touch" is done by telephone, teletype, cable, or mail. Very few foreign exchange transactions are arranged face to face. The market for foreign exchange is as abstract as the item traded in that market: bank balances themselves are abstract.

There are about twenty-five domestic banks, most of them in New York, which maintain deposits in commercial banks abroad in order to facilitate their dealings in foreign exchange. The bulk of the business is handled by ten or twelve of the great banks. New York is host, also, to some forty branches or agencies of foreign banks. Thirty-five additional foreign banks are represented in the New York market by local representatives.

The New York foreign exchange market operates on three different levels. The surface level (where the foreign exchange market meets the commercial trader) handles transactions between the banks and their commercial customers who are the ultimate users of foreign exchange. Second, there are the transactions among the banks that "make the market": dealings in this domestic interbank market are conducted through foreign exchange brokers; from time to time the Federal Reserve Bank of New York may intervene. Third, there are the transactions between New York banks and banks abroad; here too the Federal Reserve may intervene from time to time for reasons of its own—mainly to conduct payments operations in foreign exchange rather than in gold, which is getting tight.

In order to meet the needs of their customers, the commercial banks maintain foreign exchange inventories in the form of working balances with foreign banks. These balances are replenished by the purchases of balances owned by firms, individuals, or other banks; by the sale of dollars to foreign banks that may need funds in New York for their own purposes; by the purchase of bills of exchange, traveler's checks, dividend warrants, bond coupons, or any such items denominated in foreign currencies. Each bank has a staff of traders who do the actual buying and selling of exchange, backed up by a staff of bookkeepers who handle the details and maintain the records of the transactions. In a day's work a bank may purchase foreign exchange from one customer and sell it to another. If purchases tend to be offset by sales, then the bank is acting as a clearing house. Much more usually, however, the bank will offset its transactions with customers by dealing in the interbank market for foreign exchange.

The New York banks deal with each other through the services of foreign exchange brokers. Back in the roaring 1920s there were 45 foreign exchange brokers in New York. Now there are eight. Some of them specialize in certain foreign exchanges; most of them handle the leading currencies. The brokers have direct telephone connections with the foreign exchange trading rooms of the commercial banks and are in almost constant touch with the bank traders. The broker serves to bring together the buyers and sellers among the banks. For each transaction he arranges, the broker earns a commission paid by the selling bank. The broker offers two basic services. He increases the fluidity of the market, thus easing the banks' job; and he protects the names of the banks, revealing them only when a trade is completed, so allowing the banks to deal with each other anonymously. The broker coordinates the bids and offers in the foreign exchange market; he does not affect the supply or demand for currencies. Only by the oddest chance would the supply and demand of currencies match each other perfectly. The normal case is for the whole market to be a net seller or net buyer of a given currency. In that case, the brokers and the bank traders may adjust the exchange rates, and adjustments within very small limits can have profound effects on the movement of liquid funds.

Another important method of correcting supply and demand imbalances in the New York market is foreign exchange dealings directly with foreign banks. Foreign banks, operating in their own exchange markets abroad, are active dealers in U.S. dollars. They enter the market as buyers and sellers, ordinarily to prevent excessive swings in the exchange rate. Official activity of this sort is ever present as a potential factor and very often is the single most important factor in the market.

Normally, if a foreign bank needs dollars to meet the needs of its customers, and if the currency of its country is actively traded in New York, it would offer its currency to a New York bank in exchange for dollars in the hope of finding a slightly better rate than it might in its own market. Net purchases of dollars by a foreign bank from its customers might lead it to offer dollars to New York banks, i.e., to buy foreign exchange in the New York market. New York banks operate in the same way; the initiative for such bank trading between international centers may originate on either side of the water. There is, indeed, almost constant interchanging of telephone calls, cables, and teletype messages among the banks in leading financial centers.

As I pointed out in Chapter 3, the international monetary system revolves around a few general agreements. Most nations agree to intervene with central bank purchases or sales in the foreign exchange market in order to keep the exchange rate of their currencies within certain narrow limits, expressed in dollars. The dollar country, the U.S., agrees to maintain the dollar within certain narrow limits expressed as the dollar "price" of gold. It is because of these agreements, as pointed out earlier, that a general distortion has crept into the picture. A nation which perpetually buys more goods and services abroad than it sells abroad will find itself in difficulty. The U.S., as we have seen, has consistently run a deficit in its balance of payments on any accounting basis known to man. The deficit is not "settled" through the activity of the foreign exchange market as just described. The foreign exchange market accommodates actual commercial dealings.

Over the past many years the United States has spent, net, some $30 billion acquiring foreign exchange. It has used the foreign exchange to purchase imports and other goods from abroad. What have foreigners done with the $30 billion? Do they consider a deposit in an American bank as final settlement and riskless storage of value? If they did, there would be no monetary problem.

The trouble is that a bank deposit is not a universally useful form of money, and is subject to severe risks. Banks have been known to fail. Monetary systems have been known to collapse. Money, as I pointed out in Chapter 5, can lose its purchasing power through prolonged inflation. That is why, if a country consistently sells more of its money in the foreign exchange market than the market is willing to absorb, something has to give. If the currency is strong,* the foreign exchange market will bring that currency home in the form of short-term investment. If the currency is weak but the interest rate in that country is high enough to compensate for the risk of devaluation, once again there will be a buildup of foreign holdings of short-term debt instruments. If it is not attractive to invest the excess exchange in short-term instruments, it might be used to purchase more effective exchange; and the exchange rate will fall. However, the present international monetary system expressly forbids any but the smallest fluctuations in exchange rates—with the result that excess dollars cannot be unloaded at a discount for foreign exchange.

There remains the ultimate method of settling balances between nations: gold. As Edmund Wise says: "Gold has maintained its special place among metals as the accepted monetary commodity in most civilizations, and is the money used in final settlements between nations."[2] Note that *final*. In the postwar period the United States has seen its gold reserves reduced from $25 billion to $10 billion. That single fact, repeated in the light of this chapter, takes on a much more ominous coloring. It can mean only that the dollar is

* Strength in currency varies inversely with the likelihood of devaluation.

failing, and failing terribly fast, as a useful means of payment.

That is why gold becomes of interest once again. The eminent Donald H. McLaughlin explains: "Gold through history has provided a common base from which the value of materials and services of all sorts can be measured. It has provided a means for conserving wealth and making it available for useful ends. Even under the restrictions that now prevail, gold is still the ultimate standard against which national currencies are compared and it is still the one commodity in which final settlements of monetary claims between nations are made. This is true in spite of the complexities of the elaborate structure of credit and the paper pledges that serve as money in each domestic economy."[3]

Gold is interesting not only as a form of money but also as a necessary adjunct of individual liberty. No less an authority on totalitarian politics than Adolf Hitler himself came to the conclusion that gold was an enemy of the superstate; and from beginning to end of the Nazi regime the Nazis conducted a ceaseless campaign against gold.[4]

Another great modern dictatorship, the Soviet Union, feels exactly as Hitler did towards gold. It is a "crime against the state" to hold gold in Russia and in the United States. The reason is that gold, the ultimate form of money, is the only form of money which is not controlled by the state. The state can debauch its paper money; it cannot debauch gold. Therefore gold is the refuge of citizens who mistrust the state; it allows them to make financial transactions in areas beyond the reach of the state; and the state, which hates to permit liberty, therefore announces that private ownership of the metal is a crime. *Gold would have value if for no other reason than that it enables a citizen to fashion his financial escape from the state.*

It would be simply superfluous to enter into the arguments "for" and "against" gold as money. I shall have some suggestions to make along that line in a later chapter. One is not "for" or "against" gold as a metal. One can, however, be for or against monetary stability, individual liberty, and other qualities that enhance human life. At the moment I am concerned only to show what position is occupied by gold in international settlements. It is the ultimate money.

Just why it is the ultimate money is anyone's guess, and almost everyone who guesses comes up with a list something like the following. Gold is universally acceptable. It tarnishes not. It is scarce and likely to remain scarce. It is easily recognized. It is easily assayed. It is generally prized. It is easily worked. And—a quality very seldom mentioned—it is just about the most useful metal on earth, and would be used in enormous quantities if those quantities were available at a low price. All ocean-going ships, for example, should be gold-plated to guard against corrosion. All water pipes should be goldplated for the same reasons. All electrical circuits should be solid gold for best performance. Without undue exaggeration it might be said that gold is the ideal metal wherever there is no need for structural strength.[5] Many observers also say that gold is beautiful. Certainly even small children are fascinated to hold it in their hand and feel its density. How could something so little be so heavy. . . . ?

Charles de Gaulle went through the litany of gold in his press conference of February 4, 1965: "France," said de Gaulle, "recommends that the system be changed. . . . We consider that international exchanges must be established, as was the case before the great worldwide disasters, on an unquestionable monetary basis which does not bear the mark of any individual country. What basis? Actually, it is difficult to envision in this regard any other criterion, any other standard than gold. Yes, gold, which does not change in nature, which has no nationality, which is considered, in all places and at all times, the immutable and fiduciary value par excellence. . . . The supreme law, the golden rule,—and indeed it is pertinent to say it—that must be enforced and honored again in international economic relations, is the duty to balance, from one monetary area to another, by effective inflows and outflows of gold, the balance of payments resulting from their exchanges."

Yes, de Gaulle is right. Gold is the ultimate money and the only international money. It is also a metal that is finding more and more uses in industry, and this raises some interesting questions that appear to have been ignored by those economists who have been most eager to reinstate gold as a monetary metal freely circulating. But that, too, will be the work of another chapter. Let's turn for a brief look at gold itself, the metal, its characteristics, its vital measurements. It's not a little amazing.

Notes

Chapter 6.

1. The discussion of the operation of the foreign exchange market is plagiarized from *The New York Foreign Exchange Market*, a pamphlet published by the New York Federal Reserve Bank, February 1965.
2. *Gold: Recovery, Properties, and Applications*, edited by Edmund M. Wise (Princeton: D. Van Nostrand, 1964), p. vii.
3. Ibid., p. 25.
4. Charles Rist, op. cit., p. 5.
5. I owe this idea to Robert V. Jones, writing in the Summer 1966 issue of *Modern Age* ("Result Misery," p. 255).

★ ★ ★ ★ ★ ★ ★

Chapter Seven

★ ★ ★ ★ ★ ★ ★

A Portrait of Gold as Metal

GOLD is indeed a most peculiar metal. As Wilfred Krug has said, it is "one of the most beautiful of the ninety-two elements and one of the heaviest metals known to science. It is the only metal that is yellow in color in its natural state. It does not tarnish when exposed to the air and does not rust when buried in the ground. It always retains its particular beauty, color and lustre. It is the most ductible [better: ductile] and malleable of the metals. A troy ounce can be drawn into fine wire 50 miles long or it can be beaten into a thin film which will cover 100 square feet—over a thousand times thinner than normal paper. Gold is virtually insoluble and proof against nature's reagents. It is inert to most acids and bases. Its refusal to disintegrate, rust or tarnish has resulted in its being regarded as something that can be counted on to look the same and feel the same a century or five centuries ahead."[1]

Such statements are common. A mirror image is found in the prologue to William Graham's recent book: "Gold has many qualities that make it unique. It is the most ductile and malleable of all metals. One ounce can be drawn, without breaking, into a 35-mile wire. It has been hammered

121

into sheet as thin as 1/250,000 of an inch, but the qualities that make it the king of all metals are its unbelievable heaviness plus the fact it has been scarce throughout history. A cubic foot of gold would weigh over half a ton and be worth about $600,000 [at the current Treasury-pegged price; on the Hong Kong market, possibly $1.2 million]. Hence, it can be easily stored, transported, hidden, and smuggled. It is estimated that . . . all the gold that has ever been mined, about 2,215 million ounces since 1492, plus 300 million previously or over $85 billion worth, . . . would be a nugget only about the size of a large home plus a small barn."[2]

Since such statements are common, and are indeed available to the unaided intelligence, I propose to have a look at some of the more technical, and to me more interesting, aspects of metallic gold.[3] In case the reader should wonder why it is necessary to wax technical, let me explain that this clinical view of gold is intended to provide a background to the understanding of gold's rapidly growing role in modern science and industry. That, in turn, has consequences for long-term monetary policy, which we'll get to in due course. Only a bisque now: remember that it was the rapidly growing industrial use of silver that kicked the United States off its silver coinage.[4]

Far from being scarce, gold is extremely common. Hardly a rock but has a trace of gold. Workable veins are scarce; gold is scattered throughout the earth. Indeed its existence throughout the globe is one of the chief causes of its standing as an international method of payment. From the very earliest times it has been known and valued in all countries. Its unique color makes it conspicuous even in small flakes. In its natural state it is almost always alloyed with silver; the first true coins were a gold-silver alloy known as electrum and picked up from the sands of the river Pactolus, which flowed through Croesus' home town, Sardis, the capital of Lydia.

Gold is the unintentional father of chemistry. The alchemists of mediaeval and renaissance times learned a great deal of chemistry in their endless pursuit of the formula that would permit them to transmute base metal into gold. Strangely enough, modern science has been able to effect a transmutation, but in the other direction: gold *can* be transmuted into the base monisotopic mercury.*

Gold is present in sea water, but again in such small quantities that commercial recovery is out of the question at present. Theoretically such lean sources might be worked if the price of gold were raised to some astronomical figure.

Even in workable deposits the proportion of gold is incredibly small. Most of the present production comes from ores containing between 5 and 15 grams of gold per metric ton—or between 5 and 15 parts per million. Ores as rich as 20 to 30 grams per ton are being worked in five of the large new mines in South Africa; some smaller mines elsewhere report comparable ore. When gold is recovered as a byproduct of base-metal mining operations, quantities as small as one gram per ton are worked. Gravels of similar leanness have been dredged "under favorable conditions."

The gold content of the average meteorite is about 700 times higher than the gold content of the earth's surface (the deepest mines, going down two miles, are merely scratching the surface of a globe whose diameter is about 8,000 miles). There is much scientific evidence to suggest that the gold content of the ultrabasic rock and of the earth's core is much higher than the gold content of the earth's surface. There is evidence against the proposition, also: gold is only a minor component of the ores mainly associated with ultrabasic rock, and its occurrence in association with sulphides in hydrothermal deposits suggests to the experts that gold may not, after all, be superabundant in the center of the earth.

In its natural state, gold is most commonly found in as-

* I am told that modern alchemy actually has transformed base metal (lead) into gold, by nuclear bombardment in a reactor—at enormous cost.

sociation with silver. Most commonly the metal atomic alloy ratio is one part silver to five or ten parts gold; relatively pure gold nuggets are, of course, well known—but the ancient electrum contained more than fifty per cent silver.

Something more than two billion ounces of gold have been produced since 1492. Three-quarters of this production has occurred since the year 1900.

The atomic weight of gold (on carbon-12 basis) is 196.967; its atomic number is 79. Gold is not absolutely inert. It combines with tellurium. It dissolves in chlorine water and in hydrochloric acid in the presence of oxidizing agents such as manganese dioxide, ferric chloride, or cupric chloride to form the $AuCl_4$-ion. Gold is normally dissolved in a mixture of hydrochloric acid and nitric acid (aqua regia) at a moderately high temperature. Gold will dissolve in hydrochloric acid at high temperature in the presence of oxygen. Gold will resist molten alkali hydroxides in the absence of oxygen at temperatures up to 410°C (770°F). Finely divided, gold is readily soluble in alkali cyanide solutions in the presence of oxygen.

Gold is not commonly thought of as a catalyst, but it is apparently useful in making hydrocyanic acid from a mixture of methane, ammonia, and air; and in making hydroxylamine by the hydrogenation of nitric oxide.

Gold in its natural state is monisotopic. In the laboratory some twenty isotopes have been produced.

Gold has two valences, 1 and 3.

Gold has no appreciable solubility for hydrogen, oxygen, or nitrogen. It is unaffected by hot sulphur vapor. It is distinguished from all other metals in that oxygen has no effect on its high temperature behavior. That is one reason why gold is uséd so widely in high temperature devices.

The temperature of equilibrium between liquid and solid gold is 1063°C (1336.16°K or 1,945.4°F)—the highest temperature primary fixed point on the International Temperature Scale.

At extreme low temperatures, near absolute zero, the thermal conductivity of gold varies with its temperature, and not always directly. However, the thermal conductivity varies hardly at all from -183.0°C to +100.5°C.

The high reflectivity of gold through the visual range accounts for its characteristic color. Gold retains its reflectivity far into the infrared where it remains about 98.44 per cent. It is this characteristic that makes gold so useful in shielding missiles against radiant heat and in serving as a reflector for infrared heating.

Gold is substantially non-magnetic.

Gold possesses the best working properties of all the metals. It can be rolled and beaten into foil less than 5 millionths of an inch thick.

Although there are some twenty known isotopes of gold, only the mass number 197 isotope is stable. Its nucleus contains 79 protons and 118 neutrons. There are 79 orbital electrons.

The standard scale of purity is the karat. In this scale the weight fraction of gold in an alloy is expressed in 24ths. An 18-karat or 18K alloy is, then, an alloy containing 18/24 of its weight, or 75 per cent, in pure gold. Silver and copper alloys yield the red gold; copper, nickel, and zinc yield the white golds; and there are other compositions as well.

One troy ounce of gold will cover 68.3 square feet of surface at a thickness of ten millionths of an inch, or 0.25 microns. The weight of gold, ten millionths of an inch thick, on one square inch is 3.17 milligrams. For rule-of-thumb calculations, at $42 per troy ounce, each ten millionth of an inch of gold costs 60c to 65c per square foot.

Gold suffers little or no corrosion from acetic acid, citric acid, fluorine, hydriotic acid, hydrobromic acid, hydrochloric acid, hydrofluoric acid, hydrogen suphide (moist), nitric acid (70%), perchloric acid, persulphuric acid, phosphoric acid, selenic acid (67%), selenium, sulphur, sulphuric acid, fuming sulphuric acid, tartaric acid.

It suffers slight attack but is generally acceptable in ferric chloride solution plus hydrochloric acid, iodine, fuming nitric acid.

It suffers considerable corrosion with dry chlorine, hydrogen cyanide solution plus oxygen, iodine in alcohol, and as an anode where acid halogens or cyanide are involved.

Gold suffers rapid corrosion in aqua regia, bromine, bromine water, moist chlorine, chlorine water, iodine in mercury and other liquid metals, and potassium cyanide plus oxygen.

As to electrical conductivity, gold is superior to all other metals except copper and silver. Unlike copper and silver, it is not subject to sulphidation or oxidation. Pure gold is slightly softer than copper or silver.

Gold is free from the ionic migration trouble that is a problem with silver in contact with fiber and some other organic "insulators." It is also free from the tendency to form metal "whiskers" which cause much trouble in close-spaced, low-level assemblies.

Surely gold is a highly unusual metal. Its great repertoire of special characteristics must sooner or later place it in the front rank of industrial and scientific metals—as we shall be seeing in the next chapter. The time is at hand when the late John Maynard Keynes will look rather shoddy for having called gold, or more precisely the gold standard, "a barbarous relic."

Notes

Chapter 7.

1. Quoted in *Monetary Notes*, January 3, 1967 (edited by Dr. Walter Spahr; published by Economists' National Committee on Monetary Policy).
2. *The Coming Gold Crisis*, by William L. Graham Jr. (Glenview, Illinois: The Hickory Press, 1966), p. iv. In this interesting work Mr. Graham unfortunately makes some prophecies that have already turned sour. He stated with joyous certainty that the price of silver would remain unchanged "for a very long time." (P. 4.) Sorry about that.
3. The technical discussion rests largely on Wise, op. cit.
4. Modesty doesn't at all forbid me to recommend, for a view of the silver problem, my elegant *Wooden Nickels* (New Rochelle: Arlington House, 1966).

★ ★ ★ ★ ★ ★ ★

Chapter Eight

★ ★ ★ ★ ★ ★ ★

Gold: Getting It and Spending It

IN this chapter we shall be concerned with the supply and demand of gold. At the present (and since 1934) the United States has fixed the price of gold by buying and selling it at $35 an ounce. However, as we have recently seen with silver, no government can withstand the forces of the market indefinitely. In the case of silver, world demand outran world supply, and the United States had to abandon its long-standing commitment to the Western silver interests. If the picture is similar in gold, then certain very sharp forecasts can be made. We'll start with the supply and production side of the equation.

According to Graham[1], about 2.5 billion ounces of gold have been produced since the beginning of gold mining back in the pre-dawn of human history. Both because gold is almost indestructible and also because people have consistently exhibited an extremely tenacious regard for it, a high proportion of the gold that has been mined is still

128

available to human use. Some authorities[2] estimate that as much as 85 per cent of the gold that has been mined from the beginning is still "in existence"—i.e. available to human use. The only ways in which gold can be "lost" seem to be through shipwreck, ceremonial burial, unrecovered hoards, and of course the American space program, which sends its share of gold into outer space.

Newly mined gold flows into two main channels—official holdings in banks, and private holdings (which may be industrial inventory, jewelry, or savings). The accounting is the reverse of reality. In the real world, newly mined gold is bought on the market in quantities sufficient to the various private uses, and the residue is sold to the banks. In the world of accounting, there is no record of the amount of gold that goes into private inventories; the figure is reconstructed as a residual that closes the gap between known production and known changes in reserves.

In 1966, for the first time in recorded history, private demand for gold exceeded total known production. For the first time in history, the known reserves of the banking system declined.

Let's have a look at the whereabouts of the world's gold. I give below the official holdings as of year-end 1960 and year-end 1966. The figures are from the *Federal Reserve Bulletin* of May 1967, recomputed from dollars into ounces.

Gold Reserves of Central Banks and Governments
(millions of fine ounces)

	Year-end 1960	Year-end 1966
Total	1,160.0	1,230.0
International Monetary Fund	69.7	75.7
United States	508.0	377.0
Est. Rest of World	580.0	780.0
Afghanistan	1.03 (1961)	1.0

Gold Reserves of Central Banks and Governments
(millions of fine ounces)

	Year-end 1960	Year-end 1966
Argentina	2.97	2.40
Australia	4.20	6.31
Austria	8.37	20.2
Belgium	33.4	43.6
Brazil	8.2	1.3
Burma	1.17 (1962)	2.34
Canada	25.3	29.8
Chile	1.3	1.3
Colombia	2.23	0.74
Denmark	3.06	3.06
Finland	1.17	1.3
France	46.9	149.5
West Germany	84.9	125.0
Greece	2.17	3.42
India	7.05	6.95
Indonesia	1.66	0.0
Iran	3.71	3.71
Iraq	2.7	3.46
Israel	0.276	1.315
Italy	63.0	68.7
Japan	7.05	9.4
Kuwait	1.26 (1961)	1.92
Lebanon	3.4	5.51
Libya	0.086 (1962)	1.94
Mexico	3.42	3.12
Morocco	0.83	0.6
Netherlands	41.4	49.4
Nigeria	0.57 (1961)	0.57
Norway	0.86	0.51
Pakistan	1.49	1.52
Peru	1.2	1.86
Philippines	0.43	1.26
Portugal	15.8	18.4
Saudi Arabia	0.51	1.98

South Africa	5.1	18.2
Spain	5.1	23.2
Sweden	4.86	5.8
Switzerland	62.5	81.2
Taiwan	1.17	1.77
Thailand	2.97	2.63
Turkey	3.83	2.89
Egypt (U.A.R.)	4.97	2.66
United Kingdom	80.0	55.5
Uruguay	5.15	4.17
Venezuela	11.5	11.5
Yugoslavia	0.114	0.6

Apparently there are 1.34 billion ounces of gold in the combined holdings of the Communist bloc and private hands. According to one economist[3], the Communists hold about 250 million ounces. Thus the amount of gold in private hoards must be on the order of one billion ounces—worth, at $35 an ounce, $35 billion. But these figures are at best terribly inexact.

Almost all gold is mined as a primary product, unlike silver, three-quarters of whose production is a byproduct of other mining operations. The significance is, of course, that the price of gold has a great effect on the amount of gold mining activity. Although silver prices on the world market have doubled since 1961, there has been hardly any change in the total new production of silver. The same would not happen with gold. Indeed, the great rise in gold production from 1934 to 1940 was a direct result of the rise in the price of gold from about $20 an ounce to $35.

Ever since 1934 the world has engaged in one long inflationary cycle, as described in Chapter 5. The significance of this is that the ever rising cost of just about everything has included naturally the cost of running a gold mine. Labor rates are steeply up. The cost of fuel, capital, supplies, transportation, taxes, and so on is two or three times the

1934 level. But the price of gold has remained fixed by the Treasury at $35 an ounce. Consequently mine after mine has shut down, and only the newest and most efficient mines remain working. As a result, gold production is in a world-wide downward trend, which is offset by only one new development: South Africa.

The long downward trend of U.S. gold production continued in 1966.[4]

	U.S. Gold Production (millions of fine ounces)
1953	2.0
1954	1.8
1955	1.9
1956	1.8
1957	1.8
1958	1.7
1959	1.6
1960	1.7
1961	1.5
1962	1.5
1963	1.5
1964	1.5
1965	1.7
1966	1.7

Very much the same sad trend is visible in Canadian gold mining over the past many years:

	Canadian Gold Production (millions of fine ounces)
1953	4.1
1954	4.4
1955	4.5
1956	4.4

1957	4.4
1958	4.6
1959	4.5
1960	4.6
1961	4.5
1962	4.2
1963	4.0
1964	3.8
1965	3.6
1966	3.3

All other countries but South Africa exhibited the same downward trend:

	Gold Production (excluding U.S., Canada, South Africa) (millions of fine ounces)
1953	6.1
1954	6.2
1955	5.9
1956	5.8
1957	5.8
1958	6.0
1959	5.9
1960	5.9
1961	5.8
1962	5.7
1963	5.7
1964	5.5
1965	5.2

South Africa is often referred to as the one country whose gold production has been on the increase. Quite so, but even here the statistical picture is far from satisfactory. It is only the new mines that have expanded their operations. The older mines have joined the worldwide trend toward lower gold production:

Gold Production in
South Africa's Older Mines
(millions of fine ounces)

1953	9.4
1954	9.5
1955	9.3
1956	9.3
1957	8.4
1958	8.1
1959	8.3
1960	8.1
1961	7.4
1962	7.2
1963	6.8
1964	6.6
1965	6.3

During this period the world gold picture has been relieved only by the new mines of South Africa. These, working huge new deposits of very high grade ore, and incorporating all the most modern machinery and refining systems, have been able to expand their production at an enormous rate:

Gold Production in
South Africa's Newer Mines
(millions of fine ounces)

1953	2.5
1954	3.7
1955	5.3
1956	6.8
1957	8.6
1958	9.6
1959	11.8
1960	13.3
1961	15.5
1962	18.3

1963	20.6
1964	22.5
1965	24.2

It seems clear that the year-to-year rate of increase in the production of South Africa's newer mines is slowing down. The principal reason is that the era of opening the new mines is drawing to a close. The new mines are expected to continue to increase their output for the next several years, but it is highly unlikely that their yearly increases will match the record shown above, which is principally the result of introducing whole new mining operations.

Luckily the amount of gold available to the Free World has been augmented over the past few years by rather large gold sales by Soviet Russia, whose continuing inability to feed herself via state-planned agriculture has forced her to come to the West for wheat in huge quantities.

Russian Gold Sales
(millions of fine ounces)

1953	2.1
1954	2.1
1955	2.1
1956	4.3
1957	7.4
1958	6.3
1959	8.5
1960	5.7
1961	8.5
1962	5.7
1963	15 7
1964	12.8
1965	15.7

The effects of a long decline in mining activity were well described by Congressman Harold Johnson of California, testifying in 1963 before the Senate Subcommittee on Minerals, Materials, and Fuels: "Gold to most people, is California's best-known mineral. It was the principal attraction to early settlers and has continued to stimulate growth in California. Gold mining did not become a major industry in the state until after James W. Marshall's discovery at Coloma on the American River in 1848. The large output of gold from the rich virgin surface placers during the following years had a profound effect on the United States and on the development of California. In 1852, these deposits yielded more than $81 million worth of gold, which was more than 60 per cent of the world production for that year. Hydraulic mining yielded most of California's gold production from the late 1860s until 1884 when a court decree, known as the Sawyer decision, severely curtailed hydraulic mining by prohibiting the dumping of debris in the Sacramento-San Joaquin River systems. In the 1880s and 1890s extensive drift mining partly compensated for the loss of placer gold production by hydraulicking. Lode mining in California began on a small scale about 1850, and became widespread in the late 1860s. Many of the major improvements in mining and milling methods were originally developed in California lode gold mines. From 1884 to 1918 lode mines were the chief source of gold in California. Floating bucket-line dredges, which were introduced in California from New Zealand in 1898, became highly productive in 1903. California has been the source of nearly 106 million ounces of gold valued at approximately $2,415 million. This total is far greater than that for any other single state in the Union and represents about 35 per cent of the total U.S. production. Although world gold production has increased in recent years, chiefly because of increased output in the Union of South Africa and the Soviet Union [a guess?], United States production, particularly that in California, has decreased greatly. For many years the annual gold output of California was the highest of all mineral products of the state; but in 1907, gold was surpassed in value by petroleum and more recently by several other mineral commodities. Gold continued to be the state's most valuable metallic commodity until World War II. The curtailment of gold mining during World War II caused a pronounced reduction in gold output from 1942 to 1945. Following World War II, gold production rose to an annual yield of 431,415 fine ounces in 1947. Since 1947, however, gold output has followed a diminishing trend. In 1962, California's production was 106,272 fine ounces valued at $3,719,520. This compares with production figures of $4,329,000 in 1960; $8,810,000 in 1955; $14,424,000 in 1950; and $50,948,000 in 1940. This diminishing trend of gold production is attributable to several things, the most important being a fixed price for domestically mined gold—$35 per fine troy ounce—coupled with increased costs for labor and supplies. Other factors are the expense of reconditioning shutdown mines, the depletion of workable deposits, especially dredging ground, increased real estate values in some of the gold districts. At the present time there is only one major gold producer in the state. This is the Yuba Mining Division of Yuba Consolidated Industries which operates three large floating bucketline dredges on the lower Yuba River a few miles east of Marysville. The mines in Sierra County, the other main commercial source of gold in the state for the past few years, have gradually curtailed operations; in 1962 they were in the source of less than $300,000. However, several of the mines in this district, notably Brush Creek and Sixteen-to-One, have recently received U.S. Government loans to do further development work. Smaller amounts of gold are recovered from a few intermittently active lode and hydraulic mines and dragline dredges in the Sierra Nevada, Klamath Mountains, and the desert regions of southern California. In addition, some byproduct gold is recovered from several sand and gravel plants and from a few tungsten, copper, and lead-zinc mines. There are numerous weekend prospectors, 'pocket' miners, snipers, and skindivers, but the production from these is extremely small and has not offset the gradual decline from commercial gold mining. All of the large undergound mines at such places as Jackson, Plymouth, Sutter Creek, Jamestown, Placerville, Bagby, Georgetown, Angels Camp, Grass Valley, Nevada City, Mojave, Randsburg, and French Gulch are idle. Most have had their surface plants dismantled. The last active major lode-mining operations in California were the Empire-Star and Idaho-Maryland groups at Grass Valley, which were shut down in 1956, and the Central Eureka mine at Sutter Creek which was shut down in 1953. The last large dredge of the Natomas Company at the extensive Folsom field east of Sacramento ceased operations early in 1962. Now let us look at what has happened to gold nationally. The United States once was the world's leading producer, but this was half a century ago. Today it produces only 3 per cent of the total supply. . . . The United States, in a distant fourth place, has not had a real impact upon the world gold market since World War II when the War Production Board denied gold mines needed equipment and supplies and manpower. The mines have never been able to recover from the enforced idleness. Rehabilitation required great investments, and higher prices for labor and supplies could not be met with an arbitrarily imposed, unrealistic $35 per ounce price of gold which has been in effect since the 1930s."[5]

It is worth remarking that the general downtrend of gold production in all lands (with the exception of the new mines area of South Africa) has taken place even while their governments have adopted incentive programs, via subsidies for production or cost-sharing for exploration, designed to prop up the game. Such governmental supports have been instituted in Canada, the Philippines, Australia, South America, and South Africa. They have always failed in the past. It is highly likely that those who urge a domestic U.S. subsidy for gold mining operations are unaware of the general failure of such programs wherever they have been attempted.

Canada's experience matches that of California. In 1940 Canada had 140 producing gold mines, all commercially viable. By March 1964 Canada had only 49 producing gold mines, and 41 of them were receiving governmental help of one sort or another amounting to $5.20 an ounce.

All of the mines in the great Cripple Creek area of Colorado are now closed. Alaska may soon cease to produce any gold at all. Excerpts from the Annual Report of the Director of the Mint, for the fiscal year 1965, are typical: "Alaska—Output of gold again dropped sharply. The 1964 output was the smallest in 70 years except for the World War II year of 1944. The continuing drop in Alaska's gold production reflected the shutdown of dredging operations by United States Smelting Refining and Mining Company in the Fairbanks district. Virtually all of Alaska's gold is recovered from placer deposits by bucketline dredges. . . . Arizona—A ten per cent increase in gold output during the year reflected the increased production of copper. Eighty-seven per cent of the gold was recovered as a byproduct of refining copper ores, twelve per cent from refining of other base metal ores, and the remaining one per cent mainly from ores of gold and silver. . . . California—Gold production declined 18 per cent for the second consecutive year. . . . Colorado—Production of gold was up 25 per cent. Forty-six lode mines supplied 97 per cent of the total output . . . Idaho—Output of gold was up slightly from the record low established in 1963. About 60 per cent of the total output was a byproduct of base metal production, and 18 per cent was from gold and silver ores . . . Montana—Production of gold increased sharply over the record low of 1963 corresponding largely to the rise in copper output from which most of the gold was recovered as a byproduct. . . . Nevada —An eight-per-cent falloff in gold output reflected lower production of gold-bearing copper ore by Kennecott Copper Corporation. Eight lode gold mines yielded 70 per cent of the total gold output; nearly all the remainder was recovered as a byproduct from copper ore. . . . New Mexico—Gold output declined 22 per cent and output of silver was down 5 per cent. About 86 per cent of the state's gold output was recovered as a byproduct of copper ore. . . . South Dakota—Gold production increased 7 per cent and silver production 14 per cent. Nearly all of the gold and silver was produced at the Homestake mine at Lead. . . . Utah—A one-per-cent gain in gold production was attributed to increased output of silver-bearing lead-zinc ore at the Mayflower mine which more than offset decreases at the Utah Copper, U.S. and Lark, and United Park City mines. Eighty-five per cent of the total gold output was recovered as a byproduct of copper ores. . . . Washington—Output of gold decreased 5 per cent, virtually all of which was produced by Knob Hill Mines, Inc., at the Knob Hill and Gold Dollar mines in Ferry County, and L-D Mines, Inc., at the Gold King mine in Chelan County. . . ."

The relative importance of the various gold-producing states is shown in the following table:

	Gold Production in 1964 (troy ounces)
Alaska	58,416
Arizona	153,693
California	71,028
Colorado	42,122
Idaho	5,677
Montana	29,115
Nevada	90,469
New Mexico	6,110
Oregon	661
South Dakota	616,913
Tennessee	133
Utah	287,674
Washington	94,308

In 1940 there were 9,500 gold mining properties in operation in the United States. By 1957 that number was down to 1,058 and it is undoubtedly lower now.[6]

The underlying cause of this vast decline in U.S. gold operations is, as I mentioned above, the rise in the general price level combined with a "ceiling" on the selling price of gold. A graph from the 1966 annual report of Homestake Mining illustrates the point all too plainly:

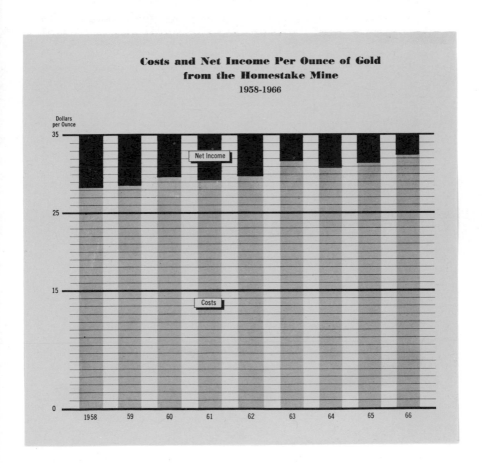

Costs and Net Income Per Ounce of Gold from the Homestake Mine
1958-1966

It requires no great wit to lay a pencil along that trend line and come up with the prediction that Homestake may have to shut down in a couple of years. Actually the economics of gold mining would dictate that Homestake keep the mine open for a while even if it must run at a loss, because of the huge expenses of resuming operations in a mine that has been shut down for any substantial period. Mines are subject to flooding, cave-ins, and other distresses. If Homestake merely breaks even with its gold operation in, say, 1969, but if it can foresee a rise in the price of gold in a couple of years, it will keep the mine open more likely than not. In any case the inexorable rise in the price level will have its effect sooner or later. And in the case of Homestake it is more than the great mine in South Dakota or the fortunes of one company that are at stake: because the Homestake mine produced 606,467 troy ounces of gold in 1966—and that's about 40 per cent of the total U.S. production. If things keep going as they are and for long enough, the U.S. might be reduced to no more gold production than we get from byproduct mining—perhaps 450,000 ounces a year. That figure is ridiculously low when compared with our yearly consumption.

Into this far from happy picture for world gold production there has recently obtruded the specter of major labor unrest in the South African fields.[7] An executive of one large South African gold mining concern was quoted as saying, "If we went only half way to meet the demands of the extremists in the mineworkers' union, eight marginal mines would have to close immediately and all mines would have to revise estimates of which ore bodies are profitable and which are unprofitable." This, in the country that produces about 73 per cent of the Free World's newly mined gold.

By then South Africa was already feeling the kind of cost-pinch that is by now universal. In 1965 fourteen of her producing mines averaged less than 70c of profit per ton of ore milled. Smallish profits can be tolerated in an industry that requires small capital. The gold mining industry is something else again. The average mine costs $39 million to open up, according to the South African Chamber of Mines. The Western Deep Mine, which aims to go 13,000 feet down, had cost $130 million and was not yet ready to go on stream.

South African gold production in 1966 rose only 1.5 per cent above the 1965 level—the smallest year-to-year increase since 1953. Finally in mid-1967 the bad news appeared.[8] The decline in year-to-year production rates, which had set in towards the end of 1966, was fully evident in the production figures for the first quarter of calendar 1967. South African mines in this period produced 7.6 million ounces of gold, slightly down from the 7.7 million ounces produced in the first quarter of 1966. One South African mining expert placed the blame on rising costs of power, transportation, and equipment, combined with the slow opening up of new mines and the shutting down of marginal mines. "If the price had been higher," said he, "a lot of these marginal mines wouldn't have closed."

The parallel with silver is astonishing. At a time when world production appears to be leveling off, world demand for the metal is on the rise. Silver production is held back because silver is largely a byproduct of other mining operations. Gold production is held back because the U.S. holds the price down to $35 an ounce. Silver's rising popularity is very much the result of modern technical industrial applications. Something of the sort seems to be happening in gold also. The First National City Bank began to publish an annual gold review in 1961. By 1963 it noticed that gold was becoming something more than a merely monetary commodity: "In addition to traditional uses, some entirely new industrial applications have been developed in recent years; the gold- and silver-plated spacecraft Mariner II, which reached its rendezvous with Venus two weeks ago, is a striking illustration."[9]

It would appear that gold is finding rapidly increased use

in "electrical and electronic components in defense and aerospace equipment and for other industrial uses."[10] The First National City Bank estimates that such supertechnical uses of gold accounted for one-fourth of the 1964 domestic U.S. consumption of gold.

Knowledgeable discussion of the new technical uses of gold seems to be excessively rare. What can be gleaned from various sources is presented here. Shannon, quoting Mac-Dougall, estimates that the use of gold for industrial and artistic purposes has been growing at the rate of 7.3 per cent per year.[11] According to Shannon, one of the growing uses of gold is as heat shield and corrosion resistant on aircraft (!) and satellites. High purity gold, which may cost as much as $65 an ounce to produce, is increasingly being used in the fabrication of silicon transistors and diodes for use in computers, aircraft, missiles, and satellites.

Mr. Donald McLaughlin, chairman of Homestake Mining, had some interesting comments in that 1965 symposium held at Tarrytown: "In the past two years the industrial consumption of gold in the United States by licensed and legal users of the metal has been nearly twice the production from our domestic mines. In the previous five years, consumption about matched production. This development clearly indicates that there is a market in industry and the arts in our country for gold beyond the monetary agencies and that it is growing. Abroad, it is not as simple to distinguish between gold so consumed and the gold that is acquired by those seeking protection against inflation of currencies [an alternative forbidden in free America], but it is perhaps worth noting that in recent years less than half of the new gold available to the free world is being added to its monetary stocks. [Private acquisitions in 1966 took more than the sum total of all new production, necessitating a decline in monetary gold reserves for the first time in modern history.] . . . In this great age of science and technology, I may be so bold as to predict that before many decades go by the demand for gold for industrial uses is going to be so much larger that gold for this reason alone in a truly free market would command a price higher than that currently defined in depreciating dollars. When the attempt is made to tie a valuable metal to a depreciated and still depreciating currency, something has to give."[12]

A recent and extremely interesting article in *Barron's* pointed up (27 March 1967) the new uses of gold (and of silver and platinum also). Gold in particular was mentioned as of great utility in spaceage electronic circuitry. The Bureau of Mines estimates that 65 per cent of domestic gold consumption is in jewelry and the arts, 23 per cent in electrical and electronic applications, and 7 per cent in dentistry. Gold is used in diodes and transistors and as small-diameter "whisker" wire. In salt or solution form it lends itself to the electroplating of printed circuits, resistors, transducers, silicon wafers, connectors, and transistors. The fastest growing demand for goldplated electrical parts comes from firms in communications and in data processing.

Says Wise: "So much attention has been directed to the monetary use of gold that its increasing application in the arts and sciences has not been generally appreciated, despite the fact that more than half of the gold available in recent years has gone into these important non-monetary fields. Indeed, no book summarizing the modern uses of gold and the properties of the more important gold alloys has been available in a form convenient to the business executive, the engineer and the scientist."[13]

Gold is useful in other fields too—measurement instrumentation, cryogenics, high-strength bonding, computers, chemistry, and medicine. A. R. Raper, in Wise p. 41, calls gold "of great industrial importance" in electroplating. Gold is used as a coloring agent for enamels and glasses. The radioactive gold isotope 198 is used in cancer therapy and in metallurgical research. It decays into the stable Hg 198, which is used in vapor lamps as a light source for precise interferometry. Gold is used extensively as a coating for grids in thermionic tubes employing a barium strontium oxide cathode. Silver-gold alloys are used in electrical contacts. The gold-nickel alloy containing 42 atomic per cent nickel is used in brazing, especially in the electronic field where its low vapor pressure is a benefit. Gold-platinum alloys are used as rayon spinnerets. Small additions of gold improve the performance of platinum in laboratory ware. The electronics industry uses 80-per-cent gold alloys (with copper, nickel) for strong, vacuum-tight joints requiring special structural properties. A homogeneous nuclear reactor at Los Alamos, using phosphoric acid at temperatures up to 425°C and pressures up to 750 psi, had all its structural parts in contact with the fuel solution plated or clad with gold. New applications of gold-lined equipment in chemical laboratories have to do with hydrochlorinations and hydrofluorinations at high temperatures. Gold has been successfully used in closure gaskets in equipment for the production of zirconium. Pure gold crucibles and gold-tipped tongs are specified for alkaline fusions and are preferred by food chemists especially in the analysis of cereal products. Gold film is used in electrically heated windshields and in electrostatic shields for instruments. Gold films are also used in windows for offices and automobiles. Gold is used in the treatment of rheumatoid arthritis and, as mentioned, in some forms of cancer treatment. The contact surfaces in telephone transmitters are coated with gold electroplate. A thin layer of gold is applied near the ends of ultra-reliable pyrolytic carbon-coated resistors made for missile use by Western Electric. Gold is widely used in instruments, radio frequency tuners, key switches, computers and relays. Gold contacts are used in high-current circuits when extreme reliability is needed along with long-term storage and where only a small number of operations are contemplated—as in vital defense equipment. Gold electroplates insure high and constant conductivity on the surfaces of wave guides, resonant cavities, tube components and other items used at radar and higher frequencies where surface conductivity is important. The interiors of the amplifiers on the trans-Atlantic cable were goldplated to avoid "whiskers," because they were expected to function at the bottom of the ocean for at least twenty years. Gold is important in transistor and piezo crystal fabrication, and in certain photoelectric and thermoelectric devices.

With such a multiplicity of new applications, and with the reasonable assumption that most of these new industrial uses are themselves in an expanding phase, it is little wonder that the use of gold as an industrial commodity has risen steeply. Although most commentators bemoan the inability to get statistical breakdowns as between hoarding and industrial use, the figures for the United States alone must be considered substantially "pure" in this regard. They make interesting reading, even if we grant them a certain vagueness.

In 1957, according to Shannon, U.S. industrial consumption of gold was 1.46 million ounces.[14]

In 1958 (using same source) it was 1.83 million ounces.

In 1960 and 1961 it averaged 2.85 million ounces.

For 1961 Wise gives U.S. industrial consumption as 2.8 million ounces.[15]

In 1962 it was 3.6 million ounces. (See Note 5.)

In 1964 it was 4.8 million ounces.[16]

In 1965 it was 5.3 million ounces.[17]

In 1966 it was 6.1 million ounces.[18]

Therefore in the past ten years the U.S. domestic consumption of gold has more than quadrupled. That is a growth rate of something like 15 per cent per year. I would guess that the great bulk of the growth must be attributable to the new scientific applications of gold.

United States domestic industrial consumption of gold is now FOUR TIMES the U.S. domestic gold production. It would be well to commit that datum to memory. When we consider that the Free World production of gold is at best leveling off and may actually decline; when we consider that the price of gold is higher in London and, indeed, on every gold market throughout the world than in New York, where the Treasury insists on holding it down to $35 an ounce; when we consider that we are supplying Treasury gold on the world market at an artificially low price when there is every indication that the rest of the world considers $35 a bargain; when we consider that foreign claims against our gold reserves are more than twice our gold reserves valuing them at the present irrational price of $35 an ounce—it becomes absolutely certain that we have entered into a monetary process that must conclude with the exhaustion of our gold reserves and a great rise in the domestic and international price of gold in terms of the dollar.

There are ways in which that denouement might be forfended. But the statistical supply-and-demand picture for gold is now exactly what it was in silver two years ago, and experience indicates that the Treasury will act late, sloppily, and in olent clouds of self-justification. From now, every official announcement that the dollar is as good as gold should be regarded as we now regard every official announcement that we had enough silver to last into the 1980s.

The day of gold as the plaything of central bankers is ended.

Notes

Chapter 8.
1. Graham, op. cit., p. vi.
2. Cf. Wise, op. cit., p. 35.
3. Lawrence Fertig, *Prosperity Through Freedom* (Chicago, Regnery, 1961), p. 37.
4. These figures are from the 1966 annual report of the Bank for International Settlements, p. 32.
5. *Domestic Gold Production:* Hearings Before the Subcommittee on Minerals, Materials, and Fuels of the Committee on Interior and Insular Affairs; United States Senate; Eighty-Eighth Congress, First Session, pp. 3–6.
6. *Gold Revitalization,* issued by same source as above (#5). Statement by Max Bowen.
7. *Wall Street Journal,* 29 November 1966, p. 32.
8. *Wall Street Journal,* 12 June 1967, p. 11.
9. *Monthly Economic Letter,* First National City Bank, January 1963, p. 6.
10. *Monthly Economic Letter,* First National City Bank, January 1966, p. 10.
11. Sir Donald MacDougall *The World Dollar Problem* (London Macmillan, 1957, p. 546) quoted in Ian Shannon, *International Liquidity* (Melbourne, Cheshire, 1964), p. 12.
12. *Gold and World Monetary Problems* (Macmillan, New York, 1966), copyright National Industrial Conference Board. P. 175.
13. Wise, op. cit., pp. vii, viii.
14. Shannon, op. cit., p. 13.
15. Wise, op. cit., p. 31.
16. U.S. GPO, *Annual Report of the Director of the Mint,* Fiscal Year Ended June 30, 1965, p. 262.
17. *Barron's,* 27 March 1967.
18. Ibid.

★ ★ ★ ★ ★ ★ ★

Chapter Nine

★ ★ ★ ★ ★ ★ ★

A Look at the Future

> Unless some solution is found to the problem of equilibrating
> surpluses and deficits, the prospects are worse than mere
> further gold outflow or bad feelings. The prospects are actually
> —in the absence of reform—for an increasing drift to controls,
> for an increasing move to autarky, toward nationalistic self-
> reliance and restriction of international trade and capital
> movements—toward all of the idiocies of the 1930s.
>
> Sidney E. Rolfe[1]

WE have come a long way since page one of this essay,
and I have yet to redeem the promise of the title. But I have
thought it utterly necessary to describe the size and make
of the various sabots in the monetary machine, if only because a knowledge of the past informs one's views of the
future. Of course one's view of the future is the foundation
on which an investment program can be erected. This procedure seems a long way round, but it is, I think, the surest.
When we get to the meat of the book, in this chapter and
the next, the reader who has followed me along up to this
point will be able to give an independent evaluation to the
ideas, forecasts, and proposals I shall be offering.

First, let's sum up the argument to this point. I bring forth
as my star witness M. Jacques Rueff, the eminent economist
who has been perhaps the closest monetary adviser to the
French banking authorities these last many years. On Octo-

ber 20, 1967, M. Rueff addressed a convention of New England bankers. This was only a few weeks before the devaluation of the pound sterling. Rueff's remarks, which I shall quote at length, invite the closest attention:

The American economy is still the most powerful in the world. The important trouble is—as President Kennedy noted in his message on February 6, 1961 [a delicate French reminder that the Kennedy and Johnson Administration have been helpless in the long run]—the balance of payments.

Some people say that this is a minor problem compared with the size of American wealth. However, it is not a matter of wealth, but a problem of the availability of foreign exchange. When a country has no more foreign exchange reserves and no availability of foreign credit, there is no other solution than the rationing of imports and full control of foreign payments, with disastrous consequences on trade and living standards.

At present the amount of free gold in Fort Knox—meaning the gold which is not earmarked as backing for the money in circulation—stands at approximately $2 billion ($13,230 million minus $11,000 million) against a net amount of at least $22 billion of short-term liabilities held by foreigners.

Of course, gold is not a magic charm. The 25% backing requirement can be reduced or waived, but if the deficit in the balance of payments does not disappear, the situation will continue to deteriorate and ultimately result in nothing less than an embargo on gold.

This explains why central banks have become very reluctant to increase their dollar balances, and some of them —not only in France—have asked for repayment in gold.

Since 1963, the share of the annual production of gold going to monetary reserves has constantly diminished: $840 million in 1963, $250 million in 1965. For the first time, in 1966 there was a net loss of $40 to $90 million.

To delay the deflationary effect of this situation and to help to finance the United States balance-of-payments deficits without too much loss of gold, numerous expedients have been invented since 1961. They are: the General Agreements to Borrow, swaps, Roosa bonds, increase in the quotas in the IMF.

Each of them has, after a certain period, become worn out. The "special drawing rights" which have been accepted in principle in Rio are simply a new step in the same direction.

With respect to the deflationary effects of a lasting deficit in the balance of payments, there is only one alternative: avoid the consequences or eliminate the causes.

The "paper gold" solution is only an attempt to mitigate the conquences by christening "gold" what is really pure paper.

All past experience, as well as the plainest common sense, shows that if the paper gold solution is applied over a period of several years, it will necessarily lead to general nonconvertibility of currencies, which results in inflation, foreign exchange controls, rationing of imports, stabilization plans and all kinds of economic controls.

Is it not awkward to see the country of free enterprise favoring a policy that leads to authoritarian controls?

If this solution is not accepted, there is only the second one: eliminate the causes, which means the deficit in the United States balance of payments.

Every year since 1961, the financial authorities have declared that the deficit was under control and would disappear 'the next year.

Experience has proved that administrative action, which means control of foreign payments, is powerless in a non-totalitarian State. If not, the United States, better than any other country because of its high economic knowledge and the loyalty of its population, would have succeeded in eliminating it.

In fact, in a free country, the balance of payments can be restored only by monetary influences such as those imposed by the gold standard when there is no major internal inflation

Of course, if this is not done through the more or less

automatic effects of gold transfers, it can theoretically be done by means of a systematic credit policy aiming at the same results on aggregate demand. But there again, if it were possible, it would have been done by the United States better than by any other country. Experience has amply demonstrated that it is politically as well as economically impossible.

Therefore we have to recreate an international monetary system in which the debtor country loses what the creditor country gains. That implies the elimination of all expedients pertaining to the family of the gold exchange standard, in other words, a return to the payment of international balances in gold.

But if the dollar balances are no longer accepted to settle future deficits, the banks that hold them will be led to ask the United States to repay them in gold. That will result in unacceptable dangers. Therefore, the dollar balances have to be repaid, at least in large part, before any return to a real system of international payments is possible.

The existing gold stocks were supplemented by the dollar balances because of the very awkward situation stemming from the fact that the price of gold has been maintained at its 1934 level, while all other prices have more than doubled in the United States since that period.

If the price of gold were restored to its previous level in relation to other prices—that means approximately doubled —the $13 billion in Fort Knox would be worth $26 billion. The volatile part of the dollar balances, which means no more than $13 billion, could easily be repaid.

The most recent criticism comes from a very important monetary authority, who said on August 21st that: "Gold as an instrument of foreign exchange is bound to disappear because of its virtual scarcity. One cannot see," he adds, "how it would be possible to get enough gold to meet the increasing need of international media of payment."

This monetary authority ought to add that if the situation is exactly what he said, it is because we have quite freely decided, against all common sense, to maintain the price of gold, alone among all other prices, at its 1934 level.

The need for gold for monetary settlements is not expressed in a certain weight of metal, but in a certain value. If the existing gold stocks are insufficient it is because the global value of the monetary reserves in gold and of the annual increment resulting from newly mined gold are only half of what they would be if the price of gold had been maintained at its normal level in the scale of prices.

Furthermore, the maintenance of a purely artificial price is an obstacle to the search for new mines and to the exploitation of those whose gold content is low.

The monetary authority referred to above added that: "There is no monetary standard more practical, more supple, more adjustable than a money based on confidence. The only problem is to extend to the international level the system existing everywhere for internal trade."

Supple, adjustable—I am afraid that it will be too much so according to every precedent of nonconvertible currencies.

With respect to assimilation with internal monetary systems, I must remark that there is a great difference: renewal of loans provides the required means for repaying. Internationally, if loans on the New York market are not renewed, they will not provide foreign exchange to repay the lenders.

In the first case, the system is self-liquidating, not in the second.

But I know the general feeling in the United States. I have too much respect for American public opinion to escape discussion on the principal points.

Is it really awkward to change the price of gold, when all prices have doubled since it was fixed in 1934? Imagine only what the situation would be with respect to wheat or steel if they were sold at their 1934 prices. What seems awkward to me is the maintenance of one price, and one only, at a level which has become entirely unrealistic.

Some people say: if done now, it would have to be renewed later on. The price of gold cannot be changed with every generation.

Let me reassure them. As long as the gold standard is

maintained, there can be no discrepancy between the needs and the existing amount of liquidity. It is only because it has in fact been suspended by a world war and 20 years of the gold exchange standard that the amount of gold monetary reserves does not correspond to the monetary needs, depending on economic expansion as well as on the increase in prices.

In such a situation, only one option is available to monetary policy: either drastic deflation, reducing prices by half, which would result in a catastrophic recession and large unemployment; or an adjustment to the new price level, which means increasing the price of gold.

There is consequently no danger that a change in the price of gold would have to be renewed, unless there were a new world war or further application of monetary expedients.

It is not true to speak of a return to the gold standard, which still exists, but only of curing the existing monetary system of the deviations resulting from the gold exchange standard.

Some people believe that a change in the price of gold would be inequitable. Is it equitable to give to anybody producing steel or coal twice the weight of gold that he would have received before the war for its production?

The change in the price of gold would diminish by half the amount of gold that foreigners can ask from the United States against their dollar balances. Is it not really in the interest of the United States, and not in the interest of its creditor, to defend such a solution?

But many people consider that a change in the price of gold would be contrary to the honor and reputation of the United States. I want to pay respect and admiration to this scruple. But there is no kind of gold clause in the main part of the dollar balances. Accepting such a clause, even implicitly, would be a free gift, entirely unjustified, to foreign lenders at the expense of the United States taxpayers.

Furthermore, the first duty of a debtor is to maintain the possibility of repaying his debt.

Would it be less offensive to repay with a "paper gold"

that would soon be made of paper only, than to recognize
the change in the purchasing power of the dollar resulting
from the doubling of all prices since 1934?

The legitimacy of such a change is so clear that a procedure for making it is contained in Article IV, Section 7
of the charter of the Articles of Agreement of the International Monetary Fund. It must be noted that it was
introduced into the agreement on a joint proposal of the
United States and the United Kingdom delegations.

Some people believe that an increase in the price of gold
would unduly favor Russia. But Russia also exports coal.
Would it be wise to reduce the price of coal in the United
States to its 1934 level in order to diminish the purchasing
power that Russia derives from its exports?

Furthermore, all information tends to show that the cost
of gold is very high in the USSR.

Other people refuse to favor South Africa. But it is generally the same people who fear an insufficiency in gold
production. It is not logical to ask for greater production
and refuse to pay its price.

It is certain that the reform will have to be carried
out. . . .

The only question is to know whether it will be done
before or after the crisis.

Let me hope it will be done before it is too late.[2]

Rueff is saying that the present form of international
monetary setlements has not worked, and that everything
the United States has done in the last seven years has been
merely expedient. He points out that gold is very different
from paper, and that the persistent deficits in the United
States foreign accounts have brought the international monetary system to the brink of collapse and the United
States to the horns of a dilemma: either institute a re-
cessionary deflation at home, or introduce totalitarian controls on foreign transactions.

But, he points out, it is "politically and economically impossible" for a modern mass democracy to discipline itself

by keeping in office the men who directly administer a painful recession. And I can find no reason to disagree with that pessimistic appraisal.

But, if we have eliminated one choice in the alternative, the remaining choice begins to take on the coloration of absolute certainty. Sure enough, ten weeks after Rueff spoke in Boston, President Johnson was forced to tip his hand. The headline in the January 2, 1968 *New York Times* is eloquent confirmation: "JOHNSON ACTS ON DOLLAR: CURBS INVESTING ABROAD AND ASKS CUT IN TOURISM."

I think we can be certain that the politically expedient path will be followed (excluding for the moment the possibility of a highly conservative President and Congress). Without going into the matter too deeply, I might point out here that the kind of action proposed by President Johnson is always self-defeating. American investment overseas is a net earner of foreign exchange, because the return on past investments is more than the amount of current new investment. Curtailing this year's investments puts a net *burden* on future U.S. balances. As to tourism, the proposal to "limit" it encouraged plenty of people to think of taking that one big trip they've been dreaming about—taking it now, before it becomes *streng verboten* under the New Economics of the Great Society. That explains why, in February 1968, the State Department reported that visa applications were running a full 12 per cent above the year-ago level.

Specifically, what can we expect in the next months and years? Voluntary programs will become compulsory. New compulsory programs will be introduced.

The "voluntary" program to limit overseas investment will be made compulsory. Penalties for noncompliance will be heavy, and will aim at corporate cash balances and top officers. Attempts to get cash invested overseas through circuitous transactions, shadow companies, cutouts, and couriers will multiply; as will the surveillance techniques of the Treasury.

As U.S. funds dry up overseas, we should expect a rise in interest rates in foreign financial centers, assuming a continued demand for capital but a relatively declining amount of capital for hire. The U.S., fearing a competitive interest-rate war, will beg the foreign central bankers to "hold the line" and dole out the credit on a rationing system instead of engaging in market transactions. Foreign bankers will pretend to cooperate, but interest rates will nevertheless rise. Foreign holders of U.S. dollar securities will begin to sell in New York and buy in Paris, Zurich, Frankfurt. The U.S. will be faced with the choices: 1) block such transactions, 2) raise interest rates here to a competitive level, 3) devalue the dollar. We will choose the second, and U.S. interest rates will rise again. That will, temporarily, stop the conversion of foreign-held assets here.

Meanwhile, the U.S. will be running enormous deficits in the domestic federal budget, and even a pronounced increase in the federal income tax will fall far short of covering the deficits. The Federal Government will be forced to borrow heavily. Part of its borrowings will represent new credit creation through the Federal Reserve System, helping to feed the fires of monetary inflation. The rest of the financing will be done in the New York money market, and will represent a huge new demand for funds. Only a portion of that demand can be met by the funds that would otherwise have been invested overseas. To coax fresh sources to open up, the Government will have to resort to higher interest rates yet again.

The Cost of Living Index, which began touching new highs at a new high rate in January 1968, will continue to rise. A rise in the price level to 10 per cent per year would not be unlikely. Already the U.S. investing public will have recognized that terminal inflation may be at hand, and there will be a rush to own tangible goods (*die Flucht in die Sachwerte*) and a swelling withdrawal from fixed-income investments. Properties covered by rent-control laws will deteriorate in price. Money-market instruments will fall. Preferred stocks, savings banks, savings and loan associations, insurance companies—all these will feel the pinch. The psychological phenomenon of a mass *expectation* of higher price levels will become a cause of the withdrawal of funds from fixed-income investments, and therefore still one more force at work driving up the interest level. In countries where the price level rises forty or fifty per cent each year, interest rates (if they are allowed to move freely) tend to achieve the same levels. Short-term money in Brazil gets about thirty per cent interest—about enough to cover the year's deterioration in the purchasing power of the cruzeiro. This would suggest the possibility of short-term interest levels reaching 10 or 20 per cent in the U.S., and I believe that the possibility is distinct. Towards the end of the inflationary boom of the 1920s, short-term money earned exactly 20 per cent on Wall Street. Just before the end.

Because of the rapidly rising price level here, American consumers will buy more and more foreign goods as they become more and more attractive in price. Once again the Government will "have to step in," to "save the dollar." There will be an initial appeal to patriotism (let us all Wear the Uniform Proudly), coupled with appeals for voluntary limitation of imports. These failing, the Government will take the classic steps: it will increase tariffs on selected articles, institute exchange controls, and introduce quotas on imports.

If foreign countries are unwilling to help finance our inflation by holding down their interest rates, I don't see why they should be willing to finance it by suffering a competitive tariff hike. So the countries most affected by our tariff hikes will hike their own tariff schedule for American products. The net effect on the U.S. balance of payments will be minimal in the long run. In the short run we will have destroyed the U.S. export business.

The exchange controls will be the opening sally in the war

against American traveling abroad. One will be required to "show a good reason" why one must be permitted to escape from these shores, the land of the free and the home of the brave. In President Johnson's first recommendations to Congress he will exclude persons on "legitimate" business, relatives going to see relatives, and old folks going home to die. Within a year or two, American travel overseas will have dried up. So, no doubt, will foreign tourism in the U.S. However, Canada will be exempted.

The Treasury will start melting its issue of silver coins.

With the domestic inflation proceeding headlong and more and more foreign commodities becoming attractive again, Washington will be faced with a choice: either put a total embargo on foreign trading, or clamp controls on domestic prices. The latter will be chosen, and wage and price controls will go into effect on almost everything. Nevertheless, a huge amount of free cash will be on hand as a result of the ongoing inflation. It will find two main outlets: black-market transactions, and loans principally in the form of government bonds. With price controls firmly established, the people will no longer fear an unending rise in the price level, and will once again be willing to put their money out for a fixed return. Interest rates will drop, possibly to the paralytic level of 1 per cent (cf. the artificial bond market of the Second World War, which lasted until 1952). However, because of exchange controls and our general economic isolation, foreign funds will not be attracted here to take advantage of the rise in the bond market or the stabilized price level.

One can make out a case, in theory, for such a chain of events arriving at a frozen situation such as I've just outlined. It is pretty much the experience of Nazi Germany. A totally isolated economy can be simultaneously inflated (infused with new credit-money) and stabilized (controlled in prices). The one great difference is that the projection I have just made for the U.S. is not a projection of an isolated economy. For the visible future we shall have large military commitments overseas, and there are certain commodities we shall always have to import. Even with the most stringent interventionist policies in domestic economic affairs, the U.S. will find itself forced to spend and spend overseas while earning next to nothing overseas. The international deficit will continue and will probably get worse.

Meanwhile, foreign markets will continue to reflect a general distrust of managed currencies. That distrust began to surface in significant numerals in the final quarter of 1967, when gold buying for individual account reached epic proportions. It was noted that the gold bought by speculators before the devaluation of the pound sterling in November 1967 did *not* come back on the market. When President Johnson "acted on the dollar" in January 1968 the speculative buying of gold was only momentarily thrown off stride. Such buying should continue, and should continue to rise.

This, of course, will bring great pressure on banking reserves. Free World banking reserves may be expected to fall more and more rapidly throughout 1968 and 1969. In similar situations in the past, a year or two of falling bank reserves would be more than enough to blow the whistle on an inflationary episode, and I would expect the same to apply again. Reserves will drop; banks will call loans and not renew others; banks under pressure will sell dollars for gold, at a discount deep enough to constitute de facto devaluation of the dollar. Washington will, as a first step, place an embargo on gold shipments—it is sometimes called "slamming the gold window down." But, under our continuing obligation to make purchases and maintain armies in foreign markets, we will have to face the drear fact that the dollar is no longer worth its weight in gold. We will devalue, and probably the rest of the world will devalue simultaneously: this is the "rise in the price of gold" that Rueff speaks of.

A rise in the price of gold, in terms of all major trading currencies, would set the stage for a general reorganization of the international monetary system, but it would do nothing to stop the perennial deficit in the U.S. payments account. We would still be faced with that awkward dilemma, the choice between totalitarianism and depression, and I see no reason to believe that we shall choose depression without first having had a go at totalitarianism. Indeed, as I write this, the President is calling for ever more vigorous "guidelines" on wages and prices.

Whether or not the real world follows this "scenario," as Mr. Herman Kahn would call it, is unimportant. The chain of events may be quite different. The pound sterling may be devalued again; the U.S. may lose another billion dollars' worth of gold in one month supporting the pound in London (as we did in December 1967); and that final loss of a billion may trigger the final run on the dollar and the final spastic efforts at defense of it, followed by the devaluation.

The important insight, as I see it, is the inevitability of 1) more inflation, 2) a devaluation of the dollar and a rise in the dollar-price of gold, 3) devaluations of other major currencies, and 4) deflation and perhaps a serious depression in the U.S. if not in many other industrial and central-bank countries.

This forecast differs from the run of forecasts because it takes into account the flipflop nature of economic and monetary events. For a dime you may purchase any number of forecasts that rest their conclusions on the assumption of uninterrupted inflation. For another dime you may fill your shelves with forecasts based on the assumption of deflation and depression. Both are right, but both are incomplete. There will be a further inflation and there will also be a deflation and recession, and any financial planning that fails to allow for both risks is in itself an unacceptable risk.

Furthermore, too little work has been done on the mechanism of financing a depression. (Yes, one finances a depression by paying off loans just as one finances an inflation by creating credit.) It is assumed that a recession will work as follows: 1) there will be a downturn in business; 2) that will cause a decline in profits and incomes; 3) that will cause a drop in federal income taxes; 4) but federal spending programs will continue at the previous level; 5) so there will be a huge federal deficit; 6) and that deficit, being inflationary, will thwart the downturn and start the nation on another economic boom.

That is simplistic. The trouble with it is that it fails to take into account the flow of funds in the U.S. economy. For one thing, there is no reason to suppose that a federal deficit, occurring in times of economic recession, must be inflationary. On the contrary. The mechanism could very well work this way: 1) there is a downturn in business; 2) as above through step 5); 6) but businessmen continue to dispose of huge cash flows due to depreciation and other non-cash charges, and government trust funds also are capable of generating cash; 7) with a discouraging economic outlook, businessmen will reduce their capital investment programs; 8) their substantial cash balances must be put to work, however, and its is reasonable to expect them to go heavily into federal notes and bonds.

The flow of funds is so huge in the U.S. economy that a federal deficit of $40 billion could be financed completely out of normal funds and would do nothing to "spark the turnaround."

So the outlook is loaded with paradoxes. We must plan on both inflation and deflation. We can conceive of enormous federal deficits and simultaneous depression. Given a totalitarian economy, we can foresee a combination of inflation and stagnation (idle cash piling up in bank accounts while wages and prices are fixed by law).

Even if the outlook were merely inflationary, without the complications and paradoxes I have tried to describe, an individual investment program would be more difficult than most people seem to think. Studies published by Dr. Melchior Palyi offer convincing evidence that in long-term inflations it is impossible to find complete protection for the purchasing power of one's financial assets.[3] During the long inflation in France between 1914 and de Gaulle's assumption of power in 1958, the franc dropped to one two-hundredth of its initial purchashing power. Meanwhile the commodity index multiplied 184 times, gold 160, bonds of course stayed flat, and common stock prices went up by a factor of 70 (those that weren't nationalized). Certain very fortunate real estate investments would have held their own through the prolonged degradation of the currency. By and large the best course was to have one's money invested in some other country.

But that option is not likely to be open to the American citizen too much longer. As a practical matter we should be resigned to the necessity of fashioning some plan for financial survival here at home. That will be the burden of the next chapter.

Notes

Chapter 9.

1. *Gold and World Power*, p. 263.
2. *Research Reports*, October 30, 1967, published by the American Institute for Economic Research (Great Barrington, Massachusetts).
3. *A Lesson in French—Inflation*, by Melchior Palyi (New York: Economists' National Committee on Monetary Policy, 79 Madison Avenue, 1959).

★ ★ ★ ★ ★ ★ ★

Chapter Ten

★ ★ ★ ★ ★ ★ ★

Investment Survival

I propose now to discuss the various main classes of investment outlets against the background of the "scenario" I developed in the last chapter. It is the contradictions and paradoxes in that general forecast that must color the suggestions I shall have about the various kinds of investments. Let me have at them, in no particular order.

Art, antiques, rare books, violins, coins. These are the Irreplaceable Object, and they have performed very well in recent years. Indeed, in certain recent years the greatest percentage profit in any kind of investment was recorded in the general field of fine art. American antiques, especially, have shown rapid and continuous rises in price. Rare books have done less well; but Americana are quite the rage now, because it appears that all the major European collections are competing with each other to build up their American civilization shelves. Old and good violins and cellos seem ever to rise in price. Everyone knows that the coin markets have churned up to all-time highs in recent years.

But: as a class, these objects are precisely the investment havens most favored in times of monetary inflation. If, as I suspect, the next five or ten years are more likely to be

deflationary than inflationary, then these objects should not
be considered a haven for capital. For they will go down in
price during a deflation just as surely as they have risen
during the inflation. In common-sense terms: suppose you
own an antique chair and, come the deflation and depression, you need cash to buy groceries. Can you take your
antique to the grocer and get a decent amount of groceries
in exchange for it? He too will be hard pressed for cash. In
hard times no one expects luxury items to enjoy a bull market. They are far more likely to suffer a more drastic decline
than the general run of prices, because they are not productive assets.

In this area, as in the others, there will be exceptions, and
I leave it to the art specialist to select one painter whose
works are likely to become the object of a "rage," the num-
ismatist to separate the genuinely rare coin from the one
that has been the target of undue speculation. As a general
rule, and for the investor who has no access to specialists, I
would unload the Irreplaceable Object at what I consider
to be irreplaceable cost today. And if you have to possess
at least one Stradivarius, why not buy one a few years from
now at more reasonable prices?

Undeveloped Real Estate. As a general class of investment, I would put more faith in undeveloped real estate than
in Irreplaceable Objects. Theoretically speaking, every bit
of real estate is irreplaceable, being unique. But the considerations of the market modify one's approach to real
estate. One is not interested in uniqueness but in unique
productiveness. Under this criterion an acre in a good school
district in Westchester should be worth about as much as a
similar acre in Fairfield.

The great danger in this area is similar to one of the
dangers in speculating in art: you may be the last, and highest, bidder. If there are traces of undue previous speculation,
you may assume that the prices have been bumped up by
inflationary demand. If you have reason to suspect that the

current price reflects a large premium over the estimated straight productive value of the property, stay clear. It is precisely that speculative premium that will be wiped out in the anticipated deflation.

Twenty years ago the best general class of real estate was undeveloped acreage around small midwest college towns. There was to be a huge expansion of these communities, and there was money to be made by putting oneself in a position to make land available to well financed institutions who *had* to have it. In scattered spots the same is true today. The general rule is: find a lonesome stretch of ground that is going to be in the way of major expansionary or commercial forces, and then don't be too greedy. Undeveloped residential property around major cities seems certain to continue to be a vanishing asset greatly in demand. I would avoid real estate investment in areas that are the beneficiaries of the "leisure time" society. That society may wake up some day and find it has to work a six-day week in order to buy bread, and there may be a sudden interruption in the trend for carpenters and secretaries to have summer lodges in the mountains or along the lake shores. Land that someone is going to *need* some day, not merely desire, is the kind you can put more faith in.

Developed Real Estate. There are two main avenues to an investment position in developed real estate. According to one plan, the goal is to hold a speculative position in the property, and the rental income plus tax write-offs are considered as compensation for the carrying costs (maintenance, taxes, baksheesh). The other plan aims not to speculate in the property but to develop it, if possible out of its own revenues, and steadily enhance its basic earning power. It is this second program I have in mind here.

Avoid those few areas where rent-control laws are still in force. Avoid areas where the population is declining (unless you are satisfied that the trend will reverse course, or unless the decline is more than compensated by an inflow of capital). Avoid overly corrupt political administrations.

Where to go? I can think of two major areas that seem to be most promising. One, surprisingly enough, is the downtown core of major urban areas. Anyone who is slightly acquainted with the great reforms that are being made in the heart of Boston and St. Louis (I pick two examples off the top of the deck) will understand what I mean. A good commercial property in a downtown area that has decided to hoist itself out of its torpor cannot fail to pay off—how handsomely depends on how much torpor was built into the price you paid and how much hoisting you can get a free ride on.

The second main area seems to me to be in the airport business. There are about ten thousand airports in this country, and some observers are of opinion that fully half of them will be expanded and modernized within ten years. This is not only a significant opportunity for people engaged in building and equipping airports; it also represents a major opportunity for investment in developed properties around those airports. (I have not included land speculation around airports, because too often the land required for runways is acquired through condemnation proceedings—hardly the road to fortune.)

Gems. These are always available as a last-ditch stand, but a moment's reflection should suffice to put them out of mind. Consider the price structure of the jewelry business. The wholesaler takes a 100 per cent markup on stones he sells to the retailer. The retailer takes a 100 per cent markup when he sells to the ultimate owner. *The retail price is four times the minehead price.* If you have friends in the business and can acquire a few "investment stones" at a deep discount from the retail price, you probably won't lose more than you would have lost in art works or fine violins. The same objections apply to both sorts of hedge.

Industrial diamonds may be slightly better than mere gems. They are at least useful in basic industrial processes, and they trade in a market that imposes much less of a markup from minehead to final user. But there are two drawbacks that seem to me to require that we reject the idea. First, if an economical way to synthesize diamonds ever comes into play, I would expect industrial diamonds to be the first to be supplanted by the new stones. Second, the price structure of the diamond trade is dictated by an international cartel, with the consequent great confusion that arises when you do not know whether you are dealing with real market prices. Economic calculation becomes exceedingly difficult.

Metals, Natural Resources. Here again we have the advantage of a commodity that is useful in basic industrial operations. Also, since most of the markets are fairly free and are the daily subject of genuine trading pressures reflecting supply and demand, the prices should generally be considered to be "true"—i.e., not unduly distorted by speculative or inflationary psychology.

The great problem is: how to establish a position? The futures markets exist primarily because processors desire to protect themselves from excessive fluctuations. The business of the speculator is to cooperate, mirror-image, for a fee. The true investor is seldom found in these operations. Nevertheless, for a spirited portfolio manager, there are few things more exciting than a dip into the futures game. It has the adornments of high margin and wide swings. I wouldn't advise getting into the futures market without long preliminary study, and even then I would prefer to hire the services of an expert adviser.

Metal bullion itself can be bought. In recent years there has been an enormous upsurge of interest in the rare metals. Ten years ago, palladium was a laboratory curiosity; today it is entering more and more into the industrial process. The same is true of platinum, silver, and gold. One might add molybdenum, bdellium, thorium—and where does one stop? Quicksilver, for example, turned in a spectacular price performance in 1965–1966.

In establishing a position in metals the important thing is to acquire what is called leverage—an opportunity to reap profits disproportionate to the basic price movement. Let me illustrate by assuming that silver goes from $2 to $4 an ounce. If you buy silver in bulk, and pay for it 100 per cent cash, you double your money. If you can borrow half of the cost, you put up only $1 an ounce, and you get back $3, trebling your money (before paying costs of storage, insurance, interest on loan). If you have bought a silver mine that cannot produce silver for less than $2 an ounce, you may make a fortune. Here again the advice of an expert engaged in day-to-day trading in these markets is essential.

Of all the metals I prefer platinum, silver, and gold for the purposes we have in mind. Gold is discussed separately in this chapter. Platinum is becoming an important metal in advanced machinery of various descriptions, and one of the major sources, Soviet Russia, is an unreliable producer. It seems certain to be increasingly useful (one of the best criteria) and at least not more abundant. In such a situation a long-term rise in price must be expected.

The situation in silver is very much the same. I think there is room for further price rises, although at $2 the price of silver is obviously less appealing than it was a couple of years ago at 91¢. Saving small silver coins is an amusing way of exerting one's independence of Big Brother, who officially frowns on such caprices, but that is all it is. There is not enough leverage in the subsidiary silver to make it attractive when compared with, say, a good silver mine. Silver dollars are different. In most of the country they have always been a rarity, a remarkable coin, something desirable for its beauty even when it circulated freely. Of all our coins the silver dollar is in fact the rarest: only about 483 million of them are thought to exist, as compared with the average mintage of

billions of halves, quarters, and dimes. The silver dollar
went into hiding in the spring of 1964 (following the Great
Treasury Raid) and will not come out again until the silver
and coin markets have settled at a new equilibrium point
completely free of governmental intervention. I expect U.S.
silver dollars in readable condition to advance in price about
15 per cent per year until the end of time, or at least for a
great many years. Over the long pull that is satisfactory
investment performance.

Other natural resources are interesting but once again
there is the problem of "getting in." Few investors are willing
to shoulder the inconvenience of buying a stand of timber
and setting up in the tree-farming business, even though
it can be very attractive. Oil and sulphur mines are nice to
have. But will oil be price-controlled? Probably. It is already
a greatly over-regulated industry. It is interesting to consider the position of oil in the autarkic-state model I presented in the last chapter. There we assumed that one of
the main dangers facing us in the long run is a shutdown of
international trade, with all sorts of barriers and counter-
measures rising at national borders. The U.S. is a heavy
importer of oil. Given a general breakdown of international
trade, I might assume that our domestic oil producers will
have to increase their production just to meet a stagnant
domestic demand. Domestic oil producers might be worth
looking into.

Prepayment of Debt. In preparation for the reversal of a
long inflationary episode, one should think about getting rid
of one's debts. The whole idea behind contracting the debts
was that they were to be paid off with "cheaper" dollars. All
very well, for so long as dollars kept getting cheaper. Now
that there is a realistic chance of dollars getting dearer, an
investor looking for a prudent outlet for his funds might
consider prepaying some of his own debts.

This might seem to be over-cautious, but I have heard
too many stories about the "surprising" bankruptcies of the

1930s to think that it's child's play to come through such an experience without at least a moment or two of anxiety. I would say that getting rid of one's debts should be a high-priority item in every person's financial planning, *unless*: debt service is a very small fraction of one's income (national average, about 22 per cent!), *or* one's income is exceptionally stable and predictable (postal worker, retired railroader).

Currency. Strictly speaking, this is not an investment. It is a pre-purchase of a convenience. If the monetary chaos I am thinking of does come to pass, there is a strong possibility that the banks will close for a while. During a banking "holiday" such as we had in the 1930s a checking account, no matter how large, is beyond the reach of its owner. It would be handy to have simple currency on hand for the small essentials of life. Perhaps the average family should think in terms of $100 in small-denomination bills stashed away in a deposit box (which *will* be accessible during a bank holiday). Collections of silver coins are an excellent step in this direction, and the face value of the silver should go towards the $100 requirement. It might be pleasurable to buy a 25c newspaper with a good old silver dime!

Bonds, Savings Accounts, Preferred Stocks. I don't see how the general class of fixed-income security can be useful to the investor come rain or shine, granted the weather outlook I have in mind. As the inflation continues, the fixed income earned from such assets buys less and less, and that loss is not compensated by any possible enhancement in capital value (the exception, convertible instruments, is discussed below). If the outlook were for a classic deflation-cum-depression following the inflation, I would agree to holding a portion of one's funds in such instruments simply as a hedging procedure—what the portfolio managers call "diversification." But there is a visible risk of general banking failures, and when such a possibility exists there is little incentive to confide one's assets to savings banks or savings and loan associations. If you *must* for your own inscrutable reasons hold some fixed-income securities, I would advise only the highest-grade preferred stocks and the highest-grade corporate bonds. It might be wise, too, to establish your position gradually, in chunks scattered over six months or a year, on the assumption that interest rates will tend to reach a peak just before the pendulum swings away from the inflationary boom.

Convertible Securities. 'This is a hybrid investment: it acts like a bond in that it pays a fixed rate of interest and has a maturity date; but it can also act like a common stock, because the holder of the bond has the right to convert the bond into a certain number of shares of common stock of the issuing company. Let the stock lie low, the bond is a bond. Let the stock rise to above the point where it becomes advantageous to buy the stock by first buying the bond and then converting it, and the bond price begins to rise and fall with the fortunes of the stock. Something has to be paid for every compromise, and the price you generally pay when you compromise with a convertible bond is that you accept something less than a top-grade piece of corporate debt. The convertible instrument is generally the lowest-ranked obligation of the issuer. It is usually issued to yield a lower interest rate than the issuer might otherwise have to pay. There are indeed risks. In this case the best protection is to invest in the convertible securities of a company that seems likely to enjoy steady growth over the years to come. Your security is not in the company's promise to pay, but in the likelihood that the company will grow so handsomely that it will have no difficulty in meeting that promise. To minimize your market risk during the first months and years of holding the convertible, you should make it a rule to buy only those convertibles that are selling near their "money" price—i.e. the price they would trade at if they were not convertible, but were merely another instrument in the money market. I believe there are some worthwhile convertibles issued by air transport companies and by companies engaged in secondary production for the home market. See your broker.

Common Stocks. Dr. Palyi's figures, quoted in the preceding chapter, should disabuse those who think that "common stock" is the answer to an investor's prayer during an inflationary epsode. "Common stock" in general does not perform very well. Given the outlook I have touched on, I see no reason to believe that you can keep your purchasing power by investing in the Dow-Jones Industrial Average. The reason is not that the DJIA is poorly constructed or that the companies will not tend to fluctuate with the fortunes of the economy. The trouble is that the principal corporations are the easiest to control politically and will be the first targets of political control in any case. We have already seen that the program of "voluntary" reductions of overseas investment was conducted by enlisting the support of the 600 largest corporations. From the bureaucratic standpoint, the ease of administration is always a central concern. It is easiest to manipulate the economy if you manipulate the few hundred companies that constitute fully one-half of the GNP. Thus the great blue chips are likely to the first victims of wage and price controls. On this ground alone I would avoid the major companies.

Another category of company to avoid is the company with a fairly stable record of sales and earnings—*even though it may promise greater things.* Once again I have in mind the danger of wage and price controls. These are always administered with a backward glance. Just as overseas investment was limited to 105 per cent of a previous year's level, so any bureaucratic attempt to administer wages and prices must look backward for its guidelines. A company with a history of stable earnings and sales will find itself in a straitjacket drawn taut by history. If, following the imposition of controls, the company should start to "move," it will have a terribly difficult time convincing the bureaucracy that its new schedules are not the result of wanton greed, wilful violations of the administrator's ukase.

On the other hand, a company with a current record of rising sales and earnings will be granted a "formula" that assumes the continuation of the visible trend. Wage and price adjustments within that framework are more easily effected. All I am doing is describing the price-setting mechanism that was in effect during World War II. I suppose Washington will wage World War III with its customary perspicacity.

There are two types of stock that will serve the purposes we have formed for ourselves: stocks in rapidly growing (and preferably small) companies, and stocks of largish companies that have enough freedom to adjust prices during an inflation and enough of a foot in the door of basic production to be in business during a time of upheaval. As to the small and fast-growing companies, I do not propose to name names; a small amount of investigation should satisfy you that they do exist. All you really need be sure of is that they will continue to grow so fast that they can take major external events in stride. The great publishing empire of Time, Inc. was founded only a few years before the Great Depression. Of the largish ones I would think of something like Quaker Oats—now there's a humble pie if ever you saw one; but it's fine on that account. If, in the midst of this country's giddiest prosperity, there is still a going market for something so mundane as Quaker Oats, doesn't it stand to reason that a depression couldn't hurt their sales? They might even grow a bit. Similar situations should yield the same results: satisfactory during the inflationary epoch, holding their own after the spasm.

Gold Stocks. This one field will bear closer scrutiny, if only because we have have devoted many a page to the position of gold. It seems absolutely certain that the "price" of gold will be raised within a few months or years. In that case

certain interesting calculations can be made with a hypo-
thetical gold stock. Let us assume that a certain mining company produces refined gold at a cost of $33 an ounce and
sells it, under the present fixed price, for $35. Suddenly the
price of gold is doubled, from $35 to $70 an ounce. Do the
earnings of the mining company double? No. They are much
more greatly magnified than that. Instead of making a gross
profit of $2 an ounce ($35 less $33), the mine now makes a
gross profit of $37 an ounce ($70 less $33). Its earnings have
gone up by a factor of 18.5 (this is called "operating leverage"). If its common stock has not anticipated this development too much, then we can expect the price of the common stock to go up approximately in ratio. Indeed, that is
what happened during the last devaluation. The Common
stock of Homestake Mining had a range of 65 to 93 in 1929;
after the rather small devaluation of the dollar in 1934 the
stock traded between 407 and 544 in 1936.

Similar calculations can be made for every gold mine, but
each mine will yield slightly different results. The mines
making the least profit at $35 an ounce for gold will clearly
show the largest improvement when the gold price goes up.
The most efficient mines will enjoy the smallest percentage
improvement in their profitability. A good general rule is
this: if you are not very sure the price of gold will go up,
then invest in the most efficient gold mines so that you will
at least enjoy some income while you wait. If you are, as I
am, convinced that a price rise in gold is unavoidable, then
invest in marginal mines. As in all comments concerning
common stocks, these remarks must be adjusted for the
prices of the stocks at the time you make your investment.
If the marginal mines have risen in price much faster than
the going concerns, some of the relative attractiveness has
obviously peeled off.

You can distinguish between the efficient and inefficient
gold mines. You can also distinguish between the domestic

and the foreign mines, and in the foreign mines you should distinguish between those in the Western Hemisphere and those elsewhere (in practice, between Canadian and South African mines). The nationality of the mine comes into play when you consider the chance of governmental intervention in capital transactions, prohibitive taxes on foreign income, nationalization, punitive taxes on capital gains (which closed down our domestic silver market for a quarter-century), and outright confiscation of foreign securities (cf. "Great" Britain).

I would guess that the domestic gold mines are least exposed to the dangers of governmental intervention or revenge, if only because it is difficult to write a "general" law that will punish only one industry. The Canadian mines are slightly more vulnerable; but Canada and the U.S. are such closely interconnected partners in economic life that I would consider the Canadian gold mines as equivalent to the domestic mines, for all practical purposes. As to gold mines farther afield, I would advise against relying exclusively on them to provide your gold mining investments. There are simply too many imponderable risks. I grant there are magnificent opportunities. The prudent investment manager has to steer a course between the best of both worlds.

Gold mines are a desirable investment because of the near certainty of a substantial rise in the price of gold. They are an especially desirable investment in the general conditions that I have been assuming. Art or antiques or coins may go up in price during the remainder of our current inflationary phase, but they will quite surely come down in price when the bubble has burst. Gold will not act that way. When, after an inflation that has lasted thirty years and affected every industrial nation[1], the price of gold is adjusted to reflect its new relation to the outstanding issue of money, a new rigidity is introduced. There is every reason to believe that the price of gold will rise and then *stay up*—which means that gold is the premier instrument for surviving the dual risks that now face us: the risk of further inflation, and the risk that the inflation will give way to a deflation and depression. The more inflation we have, the more likely we shall devalue (giving immense profits to gold miners). The greater the deflation, the greater the profits of gold miners selling their product at a fixed price while their production costs flutter downwards.

You will notice that gold mining shares, of all the possible investment answers to the perplexities of the present economic and monetary scene, are the only medium that offers a believable antidote to the twin poisons of inflation and deflation. No doubt that is why the gold stocks started moving gently in 1966 and turned in a middling performance in 1967 and have begun to attract really serious attention here early in 1968. Will 1969 and 1970 be vintage years for these rare stocks?

Let me sum up by saying that I believe it is possible for a few investors to get through the difficulties that lie ahead, but that the only way for all of us to prosper together is to put an end to the capricious monetary management that has been the fashion in Washington for these past many decades. Saving silver coins or buying a foreign gold mining stock does not amount to "betting against the Government" or engaging in similar unpatriotic gestures. On the contrary, I would hope that my comments may serve to lay open the way to financial survival for the people who are prudent enough to plan for the future. I think America stands greatly in need of people who are able to see into the future and take steps to accept it. Surely there would have been no need for this book if our government in Washington had been able to foresee the consequences of its actions. Short-sighted, foolish, and imprudent people have cooked up the chaos that lies around the bend. I would like to see the careful, wise, and farsighted come through this trial in mint condition. Perhaps then they will have their turn at guiding the policies of this country. What could be more creative and beneficent than this, to provide the means of sheltering the wise from destruction, and saving them for the great and honorable task of rebuilding a country too long at the mercy of the politics and economics of illusion?

Notes

Chapter 10.
1. See A. J. Brown, *The Great Inflation 1939–1951* (Oxford University Press, 1955).

Appendix

A Note on Monetary Reform

ONE of the sad features of contemporary economic discussion is that there is so little agreement on the steps to be taken. Orthodox economists are amazingly agreed on the weaknesses and defects in the present arrangements. Ask them what to do, say, about the role of gold, and you'll see more fur fly than you might have expected. I'll get to gold later. First let's do some doctoring on the domestic banking setup. Then let's rebuild the international monetary system. Then gold.

The great and fatal weakness of the domestic banking system is that it permits the banks to get in over their heads. The banks borrow short-term money (savings accounts, checking deposits) and lend it out for long terms (bonds, mortgages). The banks drive this easy and profitable trade until they run out of lendable funds. At that point they are ripe for the crunch. Each has a lot of depositors who can claim the bank's assets on short notice but the bank has no way to raise cash on short notice. (Federal deposit insurance programs come nowhere near covering the deposit liabilities of the banking system.) The whole subject is covered with wonderful clarity by Robert de

Fremery in the *Commercial and Financial Chronicle*, 23
September 1965, in an article entitled "What to Do about
the Dollar." De Fremery proposes that we set up a banking
system that has 100 per cent reserves—i.e., every bank at all
times will have enough cash on hand to pay off 100 per cent
of its deposit liabilities. I may as well quote the relevant
passages. The figures need no updating; the important thing
is the relations among them, not the absolute quantity of a
given figure at a given time. De Fremery:

> The Federal Reserve Bulletin gives the following figures for
> commercial banks and mutual savings banks as of May
> 26, 1965:
> $349.8 billion deposits (demand and time)
>   52.2 billion cash, balances with other banks, and cash
>   items in process of collection
>   63.1 billion U.S. Government obligations
>   226.7 billion outstanding loans
> The combined total for demand and time deposits is being
> used because, as observed by Wm. McChesney Martin,
> "time and savings deposits are in practice convertible with-
> out penalty into demand deposits or currency." He con-
> cluded "For purposes of policy determination these deposits
> should be counted as part of the money supply."
>   1) By subtracting $52.2 billion from $349.8 billion we get
> $297.6 billion—the amount of additional currency needed to
> make total bank deposits actually convertible into cur-
> rency as Mr. Martin says they are in practice supposed to
> be. (This shows why the FDIC, with total assets of less
> than $3 billion, would be entirely inadequate in the event of
> a panic in today's system.) The $297.6 billion of new cur-
> rency should be printed by the government and loaned to
> the banks. (NOTE: this $297.6 billion is not new money.
> That amount of money is already in the system in the form
> of bank deposits that exist only as book entries. The new
> *currency* is needed in order to prevent a possible contrac-
> tion of these bank deposits.)
>   2) Since the banks have $63.1 billion in government ob-
> ligations, a mutual cancelation of debt can occur, leaving a

balance of $234.5 billion that the banks will owe the government.

3) The banks would then have a 100 per cent reserve behind their demand deposits and sufficient cash to pay off all time depositors in full. There will no longer be any time deposits. Former time depositors will be asked to buy bank bonds. Banks will henceforth be borrowing long to lend short.

4) As the outstanding loans of $226.7 billion are paid back to the banks, this money will be used to retire most of the banks' indebtedness to the government, leaving a balance due the government by the banks of $7.8 billion (234.5 minus 226.7 = 7.8).

5) As the banks commence retiring their debt to the government, the government will be required to use the first $26.3 billion to retire $26.3 billion of the $38.3 billion government obligations held by the Federal Reserve System. The remaining $12 billion government obligations should be canceled. The Federal Reserve then will have a 100 per cent reserve in currency behind the $18.5 billion deposits of member banks (which own the Federal Reserve System) to enable them to retire the last of their debt to the government. (See step 4 above.)

6) All debt repaid to the government by the banks in excess of the first $26.3 billion will be used to retire $208.2 billion (234.5 minus 26.3 = 208.2) government obligations held outside the banking system. This will leave only $9.6 billion of government debt held outside the banks.

7) The Federal Reserve System would no longer have the power to alter the supply of money or bank deposits in any way. It would serve primarily as a clearing house for checks and as fiscal agent for the government.

8) The number of dollars per capita existing immediately after our banks have been put on a sound basis will be our new standard of value. We would henceforth be on a population standard instead of a gold standard. Our Constitution should be amended to indicate what our new standard is so that it will be maintained in the future.

The new result of the above steps is that over a period

of 20 years we would have eliminated $309.6 billion of a
government debt that totaled $319.2 billion without altering
the supply of money and without increasing taxes. We
would merely have given an actual existence to bank deposits that have been multiplied during the years by the unsound practice of borrowing short to lend long. We would
have put dollars where we have a right to expect them
to be.

Mr. de Fremery continues at some length discussing the
possible arguments that have been raised against such a
plan. In each case he comes up with convincing defenses.
His plan has won the approval of many bankers and of some
illustrious economists. I think it's a reasonable proposal, and
I'm especially attracted to it because of its inbuilt conserva-
tism: i.e. the plan will require a good twenty years to reach
its complete installation.

As to the international monetary system, I agree with
Mr. de Fremery's remarks (in a section of the article mentioned above but not quoted here) in which he cites the
analogy between the present unsound domestic banking
system and the present international monetary system which
allows central banks to borrow short (swaps, IMF drawing
rights, and so on) to lend long. Once again the unsoundness
of trying to build great financial structures on the basis of
abstractions and fraud is manifest. Many are the proposals
that have been made here. Because of my thoughts on gold,
I have been led to reject any proposal for reforming the
international system that includes a "return" to gold in any
official form. Instead, I would urge that we move towards
Professor Friedman's plan (it is "his" plan in that he has
become its most able advocate) of freely floating exchange
rates. This plan, in short, treats each currency of the world
as if it were a commodity to be bought and sold on a free
market: the foreign currency is merely an instrument of
trade, just as ship bottoms are an instrument of trade, and
the trading value of a currency as of a ship can be deter-

mined in free markets. I see no need for me to go over the
arguments that Professor Friedman has presented in such
profound language and also with, I must confess, a gra-
cious amiability that is his particular gift. See Milton Friedman, *Capitalism and Freedom;* and the transcript of the
Friedman-Roosa debates, *The Balance of Payments: Free
versus Fixed Exchange Rates.* My purpose in these appended remarks is not so much to argue the merits of these
proposals as to set forth in bare outline my own choices
among the many suggestions that have been made by much
more gifted observers. For the most complete discussion of
these ideas I invite the reader to consult the original
oracles.

With the domestic banking system reformed and operating smoothly, and international monetary relations being
conducted as in days of yore by the free buying and selling
of foreign currencies on open markets, there will be no need
for governmental central banks, no jobs for monetary officials
like Mr. Martin and Joe Fowler, no need for the vast institutional arrangements of the International Monetary Fund.
Indeed, as Professor Friedman points out, one of the very
real difficulties his plan must face is that it runs counter
to the most deeply held assumptions of the monetary experts of the world. These monetary experts meet monthly,
and these days almost weekly, in some foreign capital,
usually a city with good hotels, good cuisine, good wine, a
pleasant climate, lovely scenery, and the rest of the normal
equipment of governmental officials. All this travel, all this
work, these weekend conferences, these official announce-
ments, protocols, challenges, replies, programs—could it be
that they are, all of them, completely unnecessary? That is
exactly what Professor Friedman says. No wonder it is a
tough job getting a hearing from the men who have deluded
themselves to such an extent! But, sooner or later, that
hearing will be granted.

Gold. Part of the Friedman plan, as it is also part of the

de Fremery plan, is a complete destruction of the official connection between the dollar (and any other currency, if it cares) and gold. I think it is unavoidable that the technical and industrial uses of gold are going to undermine its lofty position as a monetary metal just as they did silver. It may take fifty years, granted: but fifty years is a short time when we're talking monetary stability. A monetary system that provides for stability should be conceived in terms of centuries. Hamilton's "dollar" lasted almost two hundred years. To peg the dollar to gold now, only to be forced to re-peg it fifty years from now, is precious small achievement. De Fremery's population-standard dollar is absolutely fixed, and immune to the whims of industrial commodity trading.

The great attraction of gold has been that it is impersonal, and so is able to exert a putatively non-political discipline on the money managers. But this is to shirk the issue. There is always the previous political decision to submit some decisions to the gold discipline. *That* political decision was historically possible during the nineteenth-century heyday of gold because in those times the political decisions were in the hands of essentially non-demagogic statesmen and voting classes. The will to submit to gold must exist before the gold standard may work. Indeed the will to submit to a standard must exist before de Fremery's population standard can be introduced. If de Fremery's plan has a weakness, it is there: because we have shown, in relation to gold, an unwillingness to submit to any discipline at all.

De Fremery thinks the price of gold would drop below the current official price if the U.S. were to demonetize it. I disagree. The disagreement is irrelevant, because the future price of gold has little to do with the machinery of reform as we have discussed it here. The only problem that might come up would be the problem of allowing individual citizens some kind of sanctuary from monetary upheavals. Historically that has been a function of gold, and I agree with both Professor Friedman and Mr. de Fremery that it could be one of gold's functions in the future. Both gentlemen envisage a completely free and open market in gold, and the repeal of all the present foolish laws prohibiting the ownership of the metal. We would then have an ideal situation: a stabilized domestic currency, free trading in foreign currencies, and free individual access to the ownership of gold—just in case.